Acknowledgements

To my darling Dai, it's all for you and those boys KT, Terion, and Lilo. I love you guys more than words. An extra thanks to the lady that inspired and motivated me throughout life to write/read to grow my mind, my loving Grandmother Adjua (wish you were here).

Also to the people who saw it happen:

Sheila
Zulu
Nesha
Lo
Ne Ne
Rico
Mel
Phat Kala
Mrs. Belinda (You Rock)
My Courtney
Bud
Silkk
Kelvin
Derrick (Teddy Bear)
Jacques (because you will always be that guy to me)
Cover photo: Bee & Gee Photography
Cover Model: Anganá

There's more to come so if I forgot you on this one I promise I won't on the next.

Table of Contents

In the beginning...

"I'm coming, damn," she said yelling at the front door. "I wonder who could be at my house this early in the morning."

"Hey sexy," it was Damion's too sexy ass.

"Hey," she said hiding the excitement. "What happened you're here this early? It's almost four o'clock in the morning."

"You know, I have my Syd cravings," he said with a seductive half smile.

"Stop playing, for real. What's up?" she said with an exhausted look on her face.

"Well," he said moving her out of the doorway and closing it behind him, "I heard what happened with you and Mr. Wrong at the restaurant, and if it were me I wouldn't let you go without a fight."

"Okay. What about a decent respectable hour? Like nine or ten sir," she asked turning around with her arms folded.

"Look, ma'am, I'm here," he said not bothered by her slight attitude.

"Yeah at booty call hours. Anyway, I'm going to bed now because I may have a new case or something in the morning." She yawned and walked toward her bedroom.

"No you just want to get back in the bed. Don't make up things. Chryssany…Syd? I've been with you too long," he said attempting to follow her.

"Okay, I'll show you to your sleeping quarters," she said detouring him to one of her guest bedrooms.

"I already know," he said heading to her bedroom ignoring her directional cues.

Continuing to lead him upstairs to the guestroom, she said, "Goodnight, hon. Pleasant dreams," just as she walked back out of the guest bedroom.

Syd always had feelings for Damion since about eighth grade. He had a crush on her throughout high school and she wasn't exactly interested in him; due to her being in a serious relationship. After senior year, her boyfriend Alex came out of the closet as being a gay man. This shattered her hope for her future of a happy family. Damion picked up the pieces and made her aware there is life after Alex... They had a fling that surpassed any sexual experience she'd ever encountered; it could have been because he was her first sexual encounter or how gentle he was. He had always had a friendly disposition that brought comfort and a sense of home to her sometimes coarse and temperamental character. He let her know how a woman should be treated and to never lower her standards. They never had an official relationship. They only messed around occasionally. She fell in love that summer. She never told anyone of these feelings because she didn't think he felt the same way. In many ways, she had always known how much he cared for her, but she has never had any confirmations on his behalf. Yes, he did come to her rescue, but she'd always been there for him, too. She thought that's what friends were for.

Reaching her room, she turned the light back off, The night lights came on and gave her room a luminescent feel, and candles on warmers were the scent of heaven. She finally got into her warm, soft bed and snuggled into it. She heard the sound of the upstairs shower come on an envisioned Damion's body soaked and wet under the hot steamy water. She turned on the surround sound system that led music all around the house, a soft neo soul feel of Musiq began to drown out the sounds of his muscular toned body being cleansed under the streaming hot water... She began to dose off. An image appeared in her doorway.

"Chryssany, are you sleep?" his voice whispered.

"Yeah," she said in the groggiest voice she could muster.

"Good, you're awake. Can we talk?" he asked.

"Can't this wait till the sun rises?" she said, a bit annoyed.

"No, I need to get this off my chest," he said dismally.

Okay," she said and sat up, concerned. "What's going on I'm all ears?"

"Syd, you know you were my first love and my first… ya know. I still have so many feelings for you, it's ridiculous. Some days I feel like I can't make it without you in my life. The whole 'restaurant thing' made those feelings from high school come back."

"Look D, you don't have to explain this to me. I was in love with you for a long time myself. I had to realize you and I were and are just friends, and I'd never want to destroy what we have," she said trusting their friendship was everything it needed to be at that moment.

"Would ya listen to me, woman?" he said, wanting her to feel what his heart felt that his words couldn't explain. "I need you in my life, Syd, and I cannot go without you. I need you to promise, no matter what happens, we are always going to have each other."

"I promise. Is everything okay Damion? You know I'm here for you. What's wrong? What happened?" He grabbed her face and kissed her softly, and then he kissed her forehead. She didn't know what to think. It had been a while since she'd felt this way. She noticed there was only a towel wrapped around him. She wrapped her arms around him accepting all that may happen. He untied and pulled her silk nightgown over her head, exhibiting her full naked body. His hands glided across her like a warm knife cutting into butter. He moved the sheets off her soft clean shaven legs. Rubbing her feet unhurried and affectionately, he kissed and sucked each toe and moved up her legs not missing a beat, behind her knee into her inner thighs, kissing her lips, which were also clean shaven, coming up to her lower stomach, French kissing her navel, sucking each breast gently, then placing small pecks between her breast upon her neck and on her lips. She wrapped herself around him, guiding him into her body; it was like the first time all over again. He was tender and loving as he thrust himself into her warm inviting womanhood.

He whispered, "I'll always love you Chryssany Michelle Jackson and you will become my wife."

She awakened, thinking he'd be gone, and it would have all been a beautiful dream. Instead he was there, holding her in his arms as to make good on the promises he'd stated a few hours prior. She was startled by a knock on the door. *Dang, what's this, "the make sure Chryssany doesn't sleep day" or something,* she thought.

Damion woke up at the sound of the powerful knocks on the door. Someone started yelling, "I know you in there. Come open this door and let's settle this like adults. Girl, stop playing and come to this door." She jumped up out of the bed, found her gown, and raced to the door wondering who in the hell was at her house this time of morning. To her surprise it was one o'clock.

"Who is it?" she yelled approaching the door.

"It's me, Colby. Open this damn door."

"What you need to do is, go home and talk to your wife because she ain't here. We're done talking," she said through a closed door.

"You remember that night we went to the Plush Club," he said peeking through her curtains.

"Yea vaguely. That's the night I woke up the next morning not knowing where I was or what had happened, and you said you didn't know. I didn't drink so you took me to your home and nursed me back to health or something. Why?"

"Yea well, Chryssany, I wasn't completely honest with you. We had sex that night and it was unprotected and I wanted to make sure you're straight, that's all."

"Make sure I'm straight? Let's see," she reached out to open the door when a hand grabbed hers.

His voice followed, "Don't do anything you may regret."

"Okay, Damion, what should I do? This bastard just admitted to raping me and didn't use protection, and what does he mean by 'if I'm straight?' What am I supposed to do?"

"Let me handle it, Syd. Go take a shower cause I know you and how you are feeling is an impulse to clean. So go."

"I need to handle this myself. I won't feel justified until I do, Damion. You know this. Let me handle this," she pleaded.

"Trust me, Syd. You do trust, me don't you?" he asked looking her square in the eyes.

"Yea, sure," she said as she walked away as Damion opened the door. She couldn't help but watch from the distance.

Colby said, "Damn Chryssany, either you've changed or I was fucked up from the time I met you and am just now sobering up or you just a regular ol' captain save a hoe."

"Nope, I'm Chryssany's man. You didn't know she was a lawyer and you admitted to raping her, huh? Get the fuck out and don't contact my wife again. We were going through some shit but its good now. So go on 'bout ya bidness fo' I get you some," Damion said standing as if he was ready to fuck his ass up.

Colby looked passed him, made eye contact with Syd, and she cringed and ran to the bathroom like a little kid watching her parents fight who wasn't supposed to be awake. "Whatever, man. I see you got her scared. What you do, beat her ass or something? You got the game wrong. She ain't no lawyer. She just in Real Estate. Know YO HO, I mean WIFE."

Damion stepped out the door, calmly and gently closed it behind him. He stood up straight looked Colby square in the eyes, "Call her a ho one more time, I dare you!"

"You ain't worth it. Neither is yo HO," Colby said attempting to leave.

Damion grabbed his arm, turning him so they were once again facing, and hit him with a mean right hook.

Colby picked himself up from the ground, stumbling to his car, he said, "Aight , enjoy raising my child."

"Get the fuck outta here!" Damion waved him off, walking back into the house. "Chryssany!" he yelled into the back. She could hear him getting closer. She wanted to disappear into the water. He approached the bathroom door. She pretended as if she'd been soaking for as long as he'd told her to. But to be honest, she didn't want to wash the sex off. Damion was her comfort zone and she wanted him to be her husband eventually, but who knew?

"Chryssany Michelle, did I not tell you to come and get in the tub, as soon as you walked away from that front door?"

"I did," she lied.

"Well how the hell did he see you and why do you not tell these idiots what you do for a living?"

"I don't know how, unless he can see around corners. I do not think everyone needs to know I am a lawyer or my position with the state," she said nonchalantly as she vicariously lathered soap onto her arms and legs.

"Look I know that this isn't the last of him, so what you wanna do? You can either come stay with me or I can come stay here," he said giving her an ultimatum

"I am not afraid of anything or anyone. I've been at this for almost thirty years. I can handle myself," she said submersing into the whirlpool.

"Yea," he said pulling her up to listen, "but I like handling you from time to time and I want to make sure you're safe Ms. I am Woman Hear Me Roar," he said pulling her face close to his and placing the sweetest kiss upon her lips. Taking off his clothes, he gently placed himself behind her. He caressed her body with sweet and subtle strokes from her shoulders down to her breasts and into the water right on her sweet spot. Just as round two began, her phone rang. She was about to get out and run to it, but D said, "Hold on baby girl. I got it." So she slowed down. It was time to get out anyway. Her skin had become wrinkled. As she exited the bath, she heard Damion yelling into the phone so she picked up the extension just outside the bathroom door.

"Who the hell is this?" the voice said on the other line.

"This is the man of the house," Damion said sounding irritated.

"Ain't no man of that house, so you must be the butler." Then she caught the voice it was Alex, her best friend.

Chryssany interjected, "Hey, Boo."

"Hey girl, who's that man answering your phone?" Alex said.

"Who are you?" Damion said.

"Alex, Damion, y'all need to cut it out."

"Awww, damn. What's up nigga?" Damion said.

"Not much. Same stuff, different day. What you doing over there?" Alex asked in a suspicious voice.

"You know Chryssany and her strange attraction to stalkers. The Colby nigga came over showing his ass being real disrespectful. Her 'husband' was home," Damion said chuckling.

"Don't tell me that fool thought he had a chance and you had to regulate or something," Alex asked to see what was up more than what happened between Colby and Chryssany.

"Pretty much that damn fool admitted to…"

"Well, he admitted to being happily married," she cut Damion off.

"Damn, he came all the way over there for that? I would have cut that motherfucker long, short, deep, and wide, chile. You are a better woman than me. He would still be wondering what the fuck just happened, I ain't lying, girl," Alex said mad as hell.

Damion hung up the line.

"Yea, yea, I just may be that better woman," I said grinning as I walked down the hall and into the corridor.

"Whatever, honey. I just wanted to make sure you weren't murdered during the night. Love you and I will see you for lunch, well dinner? My flight will be in later on this evening."

"I can't wait to see y'all. Where is my Shawnee Bunny anyway? I have missed you guys so much. I hate you guys will only be in town for one night. Oooh, it's gone be like old times, like high school, but not," she laughed.

"Yea, except you won't have Mrs. Brooks to fix your broken English," Alex mocked her.

"Whatever. What color you are wearing? I want to match," she asked.

"Well I'm thinking of a lavender shirt with white linen pants I got these bad shoes that would go beautifully with that," Alex said getting excited about dressing himself.

"Well, I've been itching to wear these lavender strappy, sandals. They look sort of like a wedding shoe, but whatever… I have a white sundress I'll have to accessorize with lavender," Syd said trying to get out of Damion's reach.

"Sounds like a plan. Well, let me do some last minute stuff. Just checking on you, baby girl," Alex said.

"Oh, okay. Kiss Shawn for me. Love you bye," she said

"Love you, too!"

She could hear Shawn in the background saying, "I love you, too. See you! Bye."

As she pressed the end button, Damion grabbed her from behind, and began to nibble on her neck. "You taste so good I wonder why you haven't been scooped up yet."

"I'm waiting on you, baby." she said with a giggle.

He turned her around and kissed her passionately and instantly moved down her body. He picked her up, with her legs over his shoulders, and he began to play her clit like a guitar and his tongue was the magic fingers. He laid her on the bed and came up to be sure this was all right. Again, the deal was sealed with a kiss. "You know I love you, Chryssany, and I meant everything I said to you last night." She shook her head, speechlessly. He went back down her body stopping and admiring each breast as he'd done earlier that morning. He sucked them as though it was his first time, but he was so skilled. "Your body tastes so damn good girl." He moved down to her navel and french-kissed it and crept down to her dripping wet, pulsating clitoris. He slipped a finger into her and began to clean her with his tongue.

He got back to her clitoris and sucked it as if it were his only lifeline and began to perform the "come hither" motion with the finger on the inside. Her body began to shake and shutter, and as she came he continued, only stopping to say, "That's one" He came back up to deposit his manhood into her already wanting body. He glided inside her with ease and began to work, her body begging her to say his name. She had to take control because he worked so hard that morning. They rolled and changed positions. She was on top and took charge. She kissed him deeply and passionately. She removed him from inside her and planted soft kisses while nibbling in between his neck and ear and writing her name on him with her tongue from his lips to his nipples, where she circled each three times with her tongue, and continued to go down his body, her lips meeting navel, and his lower abdomen, which made him squirm. She continued her journey to please the man of her dreams. She licked the shaft, kissed the tip, and began to deep throat him. He moaned in pleasure, "Damn Syd." She continued.
"I'm about to nut Syd." She continued to deep throat and he came. Not letting a drop pass her lips, she swallowed.

She began to lick and kiss the shaft and the tip all over again. He moaned louder. She said, "One for one." His dick became rock hard again. She mounted him and dipped, vibrated, and grinded until she felt him empty himself into her.

She was about to get off when he grabbed her hips and said, "No, can we just lie here together for a moment?" She consented. They laid there until she had another visitor banging on the door. The knock startled them both. The phone began to ring. He said, as he put on a shirt and his shorts, "You get the phone, I'll get the door."

"Okay, babe."

"Girl what the hell is taking you so long to answer the door? I know you ain't got no man, so what `the hell?" Melony yelled in the phone.

Realizing she was on her way into my room Chryssany threw on some cotton pajamas, straightened out the bed, and wet her hair.

"What's up, Damion?" she said nonchalantly.

"Hey, Mel. She is in her room," Damion said.

"Alright. What happened did he come and make a scene," she said hanging up on me, talking to Damion.

"Yea, he admitted to raping her some night. He got her drunk," Damion said.

"Damn, how she take that? I know she must have felt violated and used on so many different levels," Melony said a bit concerned.

"She wanted to kill him. Luckily, I was here because he probably would have fucked her up. Niggas like that ain't got shit to lose," Damion said.

"Shit, tell me about it. I saw him and instantly thought had to be an internet connection or a bank account connection," Melony said seriously.

"I don't know but baby girl didn't take it too well. She's in her room." Damion pointed towards her room.

Walking into the room Melony said, "Damn girl, you look awful," with a "girl, I'm just" playing smirk.

"My man ain't complaining," I said with a playful tone.

Damion interjected, "I ain't never gone complain, baby."

"So y'all together now?" Melony said. "All it took was for her to get unwillingly raped?"

"What, how you know? You told her? I don't believe this, damn it. I didn't want them to know I didn't want you to know. I don't' feel so well. Shit. I have a pain in my stomach."

"Lay down Syd. I'm sorry. I didn't know," Damion said apologetically.

"Oh, girl we got you. We've been here all this time. Everything is okay, Syd. We're like your sister and brother from other mothers. Remember? Who was there when you wrecked your car trying to work two jobs and carry twenty-one hours in school? And you ended up in the hospital, for stress. And you had all those hard-ass classes and we had to do your work and ours. Who was that?" Mel reminded her friend.

"It was you two and Alex," she said feeling a little bit better.

"When things aren't perfect, Syd, you got us. You don't have to do this alone. Know you have your people, and we got you no matter what," Damion said looking me directly in her eyes.

I love y'all," she said with a bit of remorse from not trusting them.

"Good, now get ya ass up and put on this white and lavender. They'll be here any moment."

The whole day slipped away from Chryssany. "Shit what time is it?" she asked.

"It's almost ten o'clock," Melony said looking at her watch

"Where are we going?" Chryssany asked.

"Side Street, where the best martinis are served and have the coolest atmosphere."

"Girl, don't forget about the pasta," Chryssany said rubbing her stomach.

"I see your stomach is feeling better," Damion said.

"Are you going to?" she asked Damion.

"No, you know me and Shamika are trying to work things out."

"Wow," she said in shock. "I didn't know that."

"Shit me either," Mel said, "You need to leave her trifling ass alone. After the way she dogged you, you better be glad I ain't seen her, because when I do WWF smack down."

They all joined in the laugh. Chryssany felt a bit cheated though, and the only thought going through her mind was, *What about all you said, what about me?*

"Well, bring her to my house, I forgot some stuff. Yes, Syd, I am driving, so don't protest."

As badly as Chryssany wanted to protest because her insides were screaming at the thought of allowing this jackass to lie and fool her into believing he would be her man, her lover, her husband, her confidant, her all. That was okay. She thought, *I am a grown ass woman. I'm gonna suck this shit up, live and learn. I really don't believe this shit, damn.*

"Girl, I'm cool with you driving. I got too much on my mind anyway," Chryssany said being serious and walking back into the bathroom.

"Syd, baby girl, you got me to do all your worrying," Damion said massaging her shoulders.

The first thought that came to her mind was, "Nigga get yo cheating, lying, no good ass hands off me," but her girl Mel had her back.

"Naw, nigga you got all Shamika's shit to worry about. As a matter of fact, why you get to stay here all night and day, anyway? She must be out of town or some shit," Mel said so serious that Damion' vein in his neck popped out.

"Look she ain't got me on no leash. I'm a grown man I run shit!" he said, mad as hell

"Negro, you might run shit there, but the queen of this castle demands you take some of that bass out ya voice before we all get mad!" she told him with so much attitude it could've bit his dick off.

"Damn, he getting all mad and shit. Ain't nobody here to impress D. What's up with you? Why you acting all up tight and shit? Your girl ain't nowhere around. It's just me, you, and Syd. You only get like that when you around some chic you like, done slept wit, or ya boys around. Damn, you still in love with Syd or something?" Mel said blowing up his spot.

Syd started cracking up, she couldn't help it. "Girl, if he were in love with me we'd be together, but he got Shamika's ghetto ass to fall back on. Therefore, he don't need me. I'm happy for you baby," she said turning around wrapping her leg around his and grabbing his ass.

"Y'all so wit the shit a nigga don't know why I stayed around so long. Damn, Mel you know what we talked about and Syd you know how I feel about you and how I feel about Shamika. Damn, Mel ain't you about to leave or something?" he said with too much anger in his voice for either of them to handle.

"Well, I guess that's my cue. I'm out. Is you gone bring her or not? This damn attitude making me wonder," she said looking at him suspiciously.

"I got her. It's yo ass I'm gone have to whoop," he said in a playful tone.

"Hell I don't know about that, but I'm about to get wit ya though," she said like she was about to box his ass.

"Well before anybody get with anyone one of y'all need to roll the hell on up outta my house with that stupid shit," Chryssany said pushing them towards the door.

"I don't know why you pushing me. I'm yo ride remember?" Damion asked me like we in the projects.

"Um, Negro you see them two Land Rover Evoques' out there? The black and chrome one and the white and black one? I'm sorry to remind you, the white one belongs to me," Syd said with a checkmate expression.

Mel had to add her two cent in. "And the black one is mine, nigga," she said with her ghetto fabulous laugh walking out the door.

"Damn, y'all treating me like a busta. Well, that pearl white hummer, that's me all day pimpettes," he said as a matter-of-fact.

"We know," Mel and Syd said in unison. Then they burst out laughing.

"See y'all in a minute. Love you, Damion," Mel said to squash the beef somewhat maybe.

"Love you to, Ms. Melony," he said back.

Syd walked into the house trying to think of how to ask him about Shamika without sounding jealous as hell. *Think*, Syd, *think*.

Before she could even form a thought, Damion said, "You know I only said that so Mel wouldn't make me feel like the rebound nigga. I know I'm number one and I hold that top spot and have for a long time now. Syd, you are the woman of my dreams and no one can replace you. I hope you know that these other females I fuck with are just place holders until it's our time," Damion said following her into the bathroom then into the walk-in closet.

"I hear you, Damion. Lay that shit on real thick. So when the shit hits the fan that you and Shamika pregnant and bout to get married, it will only sting not burn. Look, I've been hurt before and I have definitely had my fair share of one night stands, but you, you should know better than to play with my heart and my head. Save that pimp shit fa the hoes that don't know. Now excuse me I'd like to take a shower, so I don't meet my FRIENDS with your sex all over me," she said moving him out of the way to put clothes on the bed and turn the shower on.

"Damn, Syd. Just like that? You ain't even gone give a nigga a chance," he asked with "a what just happened" expression on his face

"A chance? Chance to what Damion? Let you hurt me? Let you cheat on me? Let you use me.........again? Na, I'm straight," she said waving her hand, trying to get into the shower.

He grabbed her arm. "Girl I wouldn't do you like that. I wouldn't disrespect you or us or our friendship. Syd, we got too much invested in us to be like this," he said with tears in his eyes.

She snatched her arm, got into the shower, and said, "Whatever D .You're happy with her and I am content alone."

"No one is content alone, Chryssany. You and I both know that. The moments we shared were truth, not just bliss. I love you wholeheartedly. I have loved you since day one, all those long fall asleep conversations in middle school. I love your hurts, mistakes, and your ability to get back up. But, you always find a way to push me away. One day I am going to stop pushing back. And you will have to be content alone," he said turning to leave.

"As long as you are with someone else, my being content shouldn't faze you. By the way, how was I going to come stay with you and your girlfriend is there? Where was I supposed to sleep in between you two?

You say you love me, but logically you can't," she said turning off the shower, reaching for a towel.

"No, there is always a place for you where I am. I don't make you alone, and you choose this illusion for yourself. Every time I try with you, there is always something," he said, handing her the towel.

"What's in the way now?" she asked attempting to look him square in the eyes.

"I just have a few loose ends to tie up," he said shifting his eyes.

"Yeah, but this is my choice. Maybe you should just go ahead and marry her. We will never have the time or the 'space' for each other. And let's try not sleeping together anymore. It only ends badly. I don't want to fight. I want to come to a resolve," she said, trying to get herself together

"But, Syd what about me?" he asked.

"What's taking so long and I thought you was leaving 10 minutes ago?" Mel said walking into the bathroom.

"I am about to put my face on and he is just leaving," Syd said motioning towards the door.

"I am leaving, but don't forget what I said," he said with a very serious look on his face as he walked out.

"Did I miss something?" Mel asked.

"No, it's all water under the bridge," Syd answered. "Mel can you walk him out while I speed this along?"

"Yeah, come on roughneck," Mel said to Damion as if he were a prisoner and she were the warden.

"Aight, now. I, well, we have to get ready, too," he said shaking Mel off. "I will be bringing my gal with me," he said with a smirk walking towards the door.

"I don't give a…," Mel started to say as they approached the door.

"She will be cool, Mel, so bring your bougie self, not the ghetto hood rat. K?" he said in a saucy demeanor, with a half-smile wanting to get under her skin.

"I'm a Gemini so we are all always here. Don't forget it," she said with a wink as she closed and locked the door.

"Chryssany Michelle, what the hell is going on with you two? Why is he all get em back, in love, and discombobulated?" Mel yelled through the house.

Syd waited until she actually got back in her bedroom. "Honey, I can't tell you about Clark Kent/Superman. He is all over the place," Syd said nonchalantly as she shrugged the situation off.

"Well, if you won't tell me, I will just have do some investigating tonight at dinner because there is something that neither one of you want anybody else to know. We have been friends way too long to not share. I have been your girl since ninth grade and I can sense something isn't right."

"You know it isn't. How the hell is he dropping me off and me riding with you? AND the Shamika trick end up invited? I just may be feeling some kind of way behind this," she said actually felling a bit nauseated. "I already don't like the female, but on top of that, did you really just choose this dust bucket over m? Really?" Syd said, an emotional wreck.

"You ready, boo?" she asked, not caring about anything Syd said. Fuck that loose woman.

Syd couldn't contain her giggle. "Okay, Miss Lee Anna. Honey, you sound just like your mom. Oh my, thank you for that. You always know what to say or do you bring my mood back up to where it should be. Ready, chic!"

Soon, they arrived at Side Street. As they walked in, Syd saw her friends and went over to greet them. "Hey, boo," Syd said with a big smile on her face. I have missed you something serious. Mel's parking the car."

"Damn, baby girl. That's all you see," Shawn said grabbing her into his arms squeezing like a brother that hadn't seen his sister in ages.

"Aw, baby, you know I missed you, too," she said wrapping her arms around him, smiling as if she had won a prize while deeply returning his embrace.

Mel entered the restaurant looking lost as hell, upset she couldn't park on the street. "Hey babe," Shawn whispered in her ear in a deeper than usual tone.

Mel turned around half startled, half wanting him to be her current boyfriend. "Damn, boo. I thought you were someone else." She kissed him on the cheek while what seemed like trying to squeeze a hug from his soul.

"Honey, we're sitting over here," Shawn said with an all grown up, "I wish he wasn't gay," smile.

Syd leaned in and told Alex, "Damn baby, you got good taste. Shawn is still the Adonis I remember him to be."

"Girl ain't he though?" Alex said gloating as he sat up gleaming with pride as his boo was literally the embodiment of what he needed in a man, hell what most women needed in a man.

Shawn wasn't always gay. He actually was in a great relationship with a woman who he thought he would marry and loved passed life itself, or so he thought. He had been with her throughout high school and their freshman year of college, but once she got a taste of other men, she couldn't stop. Shawn tried to forgive her, and even tried to move on, but kept running into trash that treated him like less than a man and cheated. He ran into Alex in college. He met all of the other friends, and had a small thing for Syd, but seeing how she only had eyes for Damion, he backed off and got to know everyone. Alex was walking to the dorms late one night and was assaulted and about to have God knows what done to him and Shawn just so happened to be there and stood up for him. He saw something in Alex that the women he had previously dated were missing. He took him to the hospital and took care of him. He has been by his side since.

"Alex I really need to talk to you about everything from Colby, Damion, and Valentino," Syd said, serious about the first two and dish-bitch about the last one.

"Child, what's up? You know you can talk to me about anything. Let me know," Alex said concerned.

"Not in front of everyone. This is personal and private. I need you on this," she said as her eyes became misty.

"Okay," Alex said.

Mel and Shawn walked to the table. "What's wrong with you Syd? Look like you about to cry," Shawn asked. "Where he at? I will take care of it!"

"I'm fine, babe. Contacts slipping," Syd lied. "Where is the waitress? I want some buffalo egg rolls. Feels like I haven't eaten all day."

"I know I want my martini and some buffalo tenders. What's been up, Alex, wit yo super sexy ass?" Mel said walking over to Alex while he stood to hug her.

"Bitch, working hard. You know the business," Alex said.

"Oh, my. Where did you park, Mozambique?" Syd asked Mel.

She said, "Close enough for you to find it when my drunk ass stumbles my way out this mafucka," she said chuckling. They all joined in with that laugh because they know it's a true statement.

"Well, give me the keys now. When you get drunk, your stuff starts disappearing," Syd said with her hand in a "give them to me now" motion.

"Hi my name is Jess. What can I get you all tonight?" the waitress asked.

"I would like a Shirley Temple, light ice, extra cherry, buffalo egg rolls for an appetizer, and shrimp and chicken pasta extra sauce. Please and thank you," Syd order as if it were her favorite song she was singing for the millionth time.

"Slow down, low down. Can we get drinks?" Alex said side-eyeing her. "I would like the drink you have with the grape vodka and red bull. The name escapes me. And may I have a moment to figure out what I'll be eating?"

"Please put my food order in because I am ready," Syd said catering to her greedy side.

"Well… since lil-hungry need food, like feed me Seymour, can I get a wedding cake and give me a moment as well to figure out what I'll be eating." Alex said side eyeing Syd.

"I would like some pineapple juice, light ice. I think I will try those buffalo egg rolls also as an appetizer, and

I'll have the steak well done dry, with a baked potato and salad," Shawn ordered.

"Damn baby, you hungry, too," Alex said with a confused look on his face.

"Yes, and I couldn't keep Miss Chryssany alone ordering while y'all clowning her," Shawn said in an "I got you boo" voice.

"Thanks babe," Syd said smiling with pleasure because someone had her back.

"Okay, I'll get your orders in. Those drinks will be right out," the waitress confirmed.

"Okay, thanks," Syd said hungrily as the waitress walked away. "Where's Valentino? Thought he was coming, too."

"Girl, you know that boy ain't got no money," Alex said laughing.

"Whoa, you ain't got to put him out there like that," Mel said shaking her head looking at him like he had a third eye or something. The drinks arrived. Mel, grabbing her drink said, "You know, if there is tea to be spilled, Alex will do just that."

"And you better know it!" Alex said in a matter-of - act tone. "But for real, he'll be here tomorrow morning. I'm ready to order."

"Okay, go for it," the waitress said.

"I'll have the grilled salmon, with a side salad. Also, I need a glass of ice water," Alex order.

Mel ordered as well. "I want some wings, mild, with fries and another drink, but this time an apple martini. Thanks."

"Be right out," she said, walking away.

"Is he bringing a significant other?" Syd asked being nosey, wondering exactly who he'd bring.

"Now you know you the only one that stays alone," Alex said jokingly but visibly hitting a soft spot, and Syd tried to play it off with a fake laugh but Mel and Shawn caught it.

"Babe, can you be a little less harsh?" Shawn said in Syd's defense as their food arrived.

"Damn real shit. That damn near hurt my fucking feelings, Alex. Hell, if I was you Chryssany I would have popped his ass a good one or at least spilled a little of his tea or something. Ugh, what crawled up your ass and died?" Mel asked picking up a one of her wings.

"Shit, my bad. Y'all got offended so I know she did. I'm so sorry, boo. You know what alcohol does to my judgment. I apologize," Alex said rubbing Syd's back in a comforting motion.

"Is there anything else I can get for y'all?" the waiter said.

"Nope, unless I can get your number so she can make all your fantasies come true," Mel said pointing at Syd as Syd smiled and winked playfully.

"Last time, Mel!" Syd said through gritted teeth

The waiter smiled and walked away.

"I thought D and his pit bull were coming," Mel said.

"Now, you know her extra ass wasn't coming and all of us were here," Alex said as he put a fork full of food in his mouth. "I knew they weren't coming because I been wanting to read that Shamika bitch since the first time she got Damion all up in his feeling. But, I am delighted that they didn't come. I would hate to whoop a hoe," he said toasting with Mel.

"Shol know what to say. Bitch would have got beat Ion give no fuck she pregnant. I got one of the best defense attorneys on my side," Mel said winking at Syd.

"So now he knows it's his baby?" Alex asked.

"Hell, naw. You know she a hoe, but you also know D is one of those guys that 'has to do the right thing.' Me, personally, would have said fuck that bitch, but of course he ain't listening to me," Mel said sucking her teeth.

"So he gone wife this trick? Alex asked with a serious look on his face.

"Um, not going to happen. Why would he wife a freak like that? She's not cute, ghetto fabulous, and all wrong for him," Syd said with a little too much jealousy to hide.

"Well, damn, I wish I had have come out the closet in high school to give you two a fighting chance. Hell, cause now he gone marry this hood rat and crush this poor baby's heart," Alex said rubbing Syd's arm.

"I think love has a way of always prevailing. You know what Mary said, 'Love conquers all,'" Shawn said with an innocent, gullible look.

"Yea babe. You keep telling yourself that," Mel said. "If love conquered all, this bitch and Damion would have been married with kids at 22."

"Is everything ok with you guys?" the waitress asked walking up.

"Yes, may I have a glass of water no ice please?" Syd ordered.

"I would like a refill on my pineapple juice, please," Shawn ordered.

"We're fine Mel," said motioning towards Alex. "But can we get the check though?"

"Okay, are any of the tickets together?" the waitress asked.

"Yeah, put them all on one," Shawn said.

"Whoa, balla," Mel said looking at Shawn, noticing Alex didn't even blink.

"What do you expect? I only deal with the best," Alex said massaging Shawn's neck.

Syd smiled and said, "I hear that. That's why ya girl right here set the standard. You start with the best and settle for nothing less."

"Yeah, I forgot about you and my love being together," Shawn said giving me a false evil-eye.

"No worries, he won't be sneaking into my room while you guys are here. I can assure you he is over me. Come to think of it, while we were dating, we were just really great friends. We seldom kissed. We slept in the same bed on several occasions. We held hands all the time, but not really much else as far as our romantic life went," Syd said reminiscently. "Okay, so I'll go get the car. We are all riding together, right?"

"Yes, we actually caught a cab here. Our things were sent to your home," Shawn answered, helping Syd gather Mel and Alex's belongings. "I'll walk with you and come back for them."

"You are a true gentleman. Are you sure you aren't looking for a wife?" Syd asked jokingly.

"Bitch you know the best ones are with trash or gay," Alex said laughing and high-fiving Mel.

"That the last shot you gone take at me, lush?" Syd said walking out.

"If I weren't gay you'd be the type of woman I would marry, oddly enough. Alex models himself after you,"

Shawn said. "As a matter of fact, your drive, in your career, how you're a hopeless romantic, and you always try to see the bright side of things. We've talked a lot about you and the things you have encountered."

"I'm not sure how to feel right now. I don't like being the topic of anyone's conversation, but I appreciate the adoration," she said feeling a bit uneasy. She hit the keyless entry and Shawn opened the door. She thought for a split second about what to say when he got in. Opening the door, she said, "Without Alex, I would still be a timid 'yes' girl. He taught me to speak my mind and express myself without crying. It seems simple enough now, but back then, it was my only recourse."

"I understand, honey. He has that 'I am a grown up complex 'and has no problem letting ANYBODY know it," Shawn said with a laugh. "Be right back."

"Damn, that was fast," Mel said. "Tell that bitch don't get no ticket in my car speeding. I ain't playing either, hell."

"She always drives like we Miss Daisy anyways. If she get a ticket, it's because yo ass doing something stupid," Alex said walking with more than a little prance.

"Up we go," Shawn instructed Mel.

"Uh uh, I am getting in the back so I can stretch out," Mel said turning around and opening the backdoor.

"Okay, babe?" Shawn gestured for Alex to ride in the front.

"Nope, backseat shawty. This lush needs leaning room," Alex said climbing into the backseat.

"It was so much fun catching up with y'all. When y'all coming back?" Mel said.

"Well, Ms. Thang, we should be back in about four or five months. Hopefully you will have gotten over this hangover," Shawn said chuckling.

"Yeah, honey. When you stop knowing how to hold your liquor? We used to drink all night and day and still be cool. You getting old, girlie," Alex said to Mel.

"Y'all get off my sister," Syd said looking straight ahead.

Syd's phone rang, her Erykah Badu "Next Lifetime" ringtone filling the car. Mel, Shawn, and Alex said, "HEY DAMION!" in unison.

She couldn't even lie and say it wasn't him. "Hey, what's up?" she said blushing and answering the phone.

"Where y'all at?" Damion said.

"We're leaving the restaurant. You know. it was nice seeing the both of you. Didn't think we'd enjoy Shamika's presence, but it was like neither of you were even there ya know?" she said in a facetious tone to be petty because she knew she had back up.

Chuckling Damion said, "Alright cut the crap Syd. I get it. You know how Mika is and how y'all are! I couldn't put myself through that, and I know you don't like to see us together."

"I am so over that," she said in an almost honest tone. "But, we were expecting you, you know, to catch up and do the things that childhood friends do, I guess we understand."

"I'on understand shit. That ghetto ass bitch got you fucked up. You all wrapped around her ratchet ass finger. Never thought you would be the product of entrapment," Mel said making everyone in the car laugh.

The call was on Bluetooth in the car. "Guess you heard that," Syd said muffling her laugh.

"You know what? Fuck all y'all!" Damion said in a bitter tone.

"See, I was gone just let this bitch read you, but you had to say ALL, so here's my 'T' for you, hope it ain't too hot. Word on the street yo baby momma ain't yours no way. She pregnant by a dude in the hood, but met you and fucked, now she living the good life. Soooooo, you might want to stop fucking people," Alex said sucking his teeth.

"Alex, why would you? I don't understand. Tact! This wasn't the time or place. Why?" Syd asked a bit taken aback by all the shade thrown.

"Well, let your sources know I got this, and get they're shit checked, before someone finds out about your little secrets. As a matter of fact, where is good ole, Valentino?" Damion asked before rudely disconnecting the call.

Mel sat up saying with a slight laugh, "I guess his ol' ball and chain, done pissed on his parade."

"Yea, honey I guess", Alex said summing up Damion's comment.

Shawn, drove to the Double Tree, where they'd previously made reservations. "Here we are." He said as he pulled up to the door, and helped Alex out the truck.

"Okay, babe, see you two in the morning." Syd said hugging and kissing them both on their cheeks.

"Be safe, honey" Shawn said as he walked he and Alex in the double doors.

Syd looked back to find her friend fast asleep on the back seat, *I guess you're spending the night,* she thought as she began her drive home.

Alex and Shawn

"We are on our way, honey. Keep your pants on, damn," Chryssany said sarcastically.

"If you come alone, I promise to take yours off slowly," Damion said in a seductive voice.

She laughed and asked, "So how is Mika doing these days? As a matter of fact tell her I said hello."

"So how close are y'all?" he said in an "I get it voice."

"We are getting off on your exit now. You better be ready, too," she said in a stern voice.

"I am ready and trying to leave before Mika gets here," he said in a hurry up voice.

Shawn turned the corner and made Chryssany kind of nauseous. "Whoa, can we go easy on the turns please?" Syd said. "And please hurry up and get me to a restroom."

"Okay boo, we almost there," Shawn said and winked at her in the rearview mirror.

"Thanks," she said clutching her stomach.

Mel sat up and said, "Um huh."

"Okay Damion, we're almost there," Chryssany, said trying to get him off the phone before Mel began nagging about anything.

"Aight, I think I see y'all coming into the estates anyway," Damion said.

"Yeah, that's us. Open the door. I need to use the restroom," she said.

"Me too," Mel yelled into the phone.

"Okay, it's open," he said opening the door.

They pulled up into his 180 degree driveway. Chryssany almost made a new door in Shawn's rented Navigator before the truck stopped completely, jumping out to get to the restroom. She ran passed Damion straight into his Amarillo alga, limestone guest restroom down the hall in front of the entrance way. Mel got out slowly with Damion's help and found her way and her friend in the restroom vomiting her heart out. "Girl, what the hell wrong with you?" she said pulling her friend's hair back into a bun.

"I don't know. This just started this morning, I think I can shake it. I'll be fine," Syd said shaking it off.

"Okay fine, you might be pregnant," she said jokingly.

"Whatever, that damn food messed me up last night, that's all," she said one-hundred percent positive it was the food.

"Aight, you done? I gotta pee bad as hell," she said doing the pee pee dance.

"Yeah I am," she said getting up, washing her hands, face, and rinsing her mouth out. She fixed her clothes and lip gloss.

"I bet you won't drink like that again," Chryssany said laughing at Mel, who was slightly falling off the toilet. Mel couldn't say anything so she just flipped her the bird, making her laugh.

"Hey, y'all alright in there?" Damion yelled.

"Yeah, we're fine. On our way out," Syd yelled back.

Mel washed her hands and walked back to the truck while Syd stayed behind to be sure she cleared the mess. Damion walk in and asked, "Hey, baby girl. You sure you okay? I heard you regurgitating and if you need anything let me know."

"No, I am fine. Seriously, Damion it was something I ate last night and I am positive. Thanks anyways boo," she said with a wink.

"I was serious about them pants, too. Why you trying to ignore me? I ain't forgot, lil mama," he said rubbing her back.

"Whatever, lil daddy," she said with a smile, walking out the door.

"Why are we all smiles and I owe you an ass whooping, Damion. I know you were the one my girl cheated with sucka!" Alex yelled out the window playfully.

Damion, locking the door said, "Nigga, if you was putting it down right, she wouldn't have had to come to big daddy. Ain't that right baby?" he said stroking her hair.

"Baby, he got me drunk and made me sign an agreement to love him forever and never speak of it again, I promise," Chryssany said grabbing Alex's arms.

"Okay, honey, you move your meat you lose your seat, and now he has a new seat so hands off, cutie," Shawn said smiling.

"Okay, sorry. I'll get my ass in the backseat this time," Syd said getting off Alex's lap and into the backseat.

"Um, I got a seat for you right here baby," Damion said patting his lap with his bright smile and deep dimples.

"No thanks, lil daddy. I'll sit on the seat," Syd said sitting next to him.

"So, Chryssany you peeing and throwing up an awful lot. Who's the lucky man, cause it can't be just the food," Shawn said looking in the rearview mirror.

"Bitch, please. That scanty woman ain't pregnant and ain't told her best friend in the whole world. Ain't that right, boo?" Alex said winking at Syd like he just knew.

"Wait a minute with the best friend shit. I get offended, you know. She was mine before y'all two were a couple let alone friends," Mel said raising her head up out of Syd's lap. "Ain't that right, Ms. Thang?"

"You're right, Mel. Now stop moving so much. There's not enough room for all that," she said trying to get back into a tolerable position.

"Well, if we wanna go back in time I do believe I was her friend first," Damion said with a reminiscing look on his face.

"In your mind," Mel and Alex said in unison, and they all burst out laughing.

Damion not thinking it's was so funny asked, "Are we there yet?"

"Aw, baby, don't get defensive. You were my first something so that's fine," she whispered into Damion's ear.

He smiled and crossed his legs trying, to hide his erection.

"Look if you gone whisper, do it right. I heard you, and we all knew that anyway," Mel said in a drunken slur.

As Shawn pulled into the airport, Syd's eyes began to tear up. "I am not ready. You should have left me at home. "

"Oh, honey, it's just for a little while," Alex said turning around to rub her hands.

"Plus you still have me," Damion said jokingly.

That statement only made her cry harder because he was a low down dirty scoundrel who stole her heart, made her love him, and gave him her goodies just for him to leave her high and dry; like he always did!

"Look Damion, we all know the business between you two so please don't't' help the situation because when you're done 'fixing' things, you still have to trot your happy ass back into your perfect little ghetto ass family life so shut the fuck up and let her cry about them leaving and not you leaving in the future, thanks," Mel said sick of her best friend's mood swings.

"Ugh, whatever. Mel, take yo drunk ass back to sleep. You don't know what you talking about!" Damion said aggressively.

"Damn, y'all gone make us miss our flight, spilling the tea like that," Alex said meddling.

"We can always reschedule," Shawn said fooling around.

Alex began to think, just before he said, "Okay, we'll stay a little longer. If it's ok ay with you?" He looked at Shawn with the kindest baby face.

Shawn simply said, "Who could say no to that face?", as he pulled out of the airport and headed back to the Doubletree hotel.

Valentino

After dropping everyone off, Syd pulled into her driveway, pressing the garage opener. She thought she saw a man sitting in the bushes. She said to herself, "But it's been a long night and I will not call the police again for a bush." Her truck lowered and she got out, closed the door, and hit the alarm. "My neighbors can't see me if I enter my house through the garage and frankly I am afraid of the dark," she thought. She walked up to her door, slightly humming "Amazing Grace," her comfort song. She wrapped her hands around the mace on her keychain, just in case there was a man in the bushes this time. She giggled a little from the last time. No man, only grass. She pulled her key up to the lock.

"I hope that mace ain't yo only line of defense," a deep voice said from the bushes.

"Jesus, Jesus, Jesus," Syd said.

"Calm down lil scary," Valentino came out the bushes. "I had to hide. Yo neighbors nosey as hell, and you know they called the police on me last time!"

"Ass that was messed up. I thought you weren't getting back until morning," she asked, breathing a sigh of relief.

"Nah, I got on the train instead of the greyhound. Got me here that much faster," he said walking in the house behind her. "You gone turn the alarm off," he asked with his arms out stretched.

"I already did, from my keychain," she said, raising it, before laying it on the counter and falling into his arms. "Man, you missed a great dinner, but we'll talk about that in the morning. Everyone is coming over for breakfast," she said, getting herself ready for a shower and bed. "If you do anything in my house this time, I will shank you! I'm not playing," she said through a fake smile.

"That's what's up, a'ight, damn Syd, but I understand. I'm gone let you do yo thang. Goodnight love." He walked over and hugged her tight and kissed her forehead.

"Love you much honey," she said returning his embrace.

He walked out and she hit the shower and to bed she went.

"Girl, wake up yo company outside," Mel said plopping into the other side of Syd's bed. "Alex said he ain't coming in until you come get him. D was right behind me."

"I'm taking my damn keys back, ugh," Syd said, waking up a little annoyed, but more excited, getting up to go get Alex, real extra ass.

"Hey you," Syd said, walking outside greeting Alex.

"Bitch, you know I should have got on that flight yesterday. I can't deal with this shit.

If I lose my man, I will kill you and that baby you think I don't know about.

Grow some common sense. You stay fucking this dude raw as hell, then you all of a sudden sick, throwing up and shit. Bitch, please be logical girl. Some shit just makes sense. I swear sometimes I don't know how you became a lawyer," Alex said walking her into the house, holding her arm tighter than comfortable.

"Let me go," she whispered. "First of all, this is your shit to deal with, not mine. As you recall, I wasn't in the room you two were. And how dare you threaten me with your garbage? Bitch he deserves someone who wouldn't do that to him, not someone with your sorted past. Don't ever try to read me Miss Bitch because I wrote the fucking book. Now go have several seats before I blow your spot up. Furthermore what this vagina does is none of your concern," she said turning to walk away.

"Okay, so you might have a lil phi to you, but don't push it. Love you too scary spice," Alex said trying to clear the air but it was still very bitter.

"No worries, just don't come for me. I do this," she said snapping and rolling her neck, not really acknowledging his apology. "Love you, too, though," she said over her shoulder with a smile and a wink. They walked in the front door and Valentino froze as he made eye contact. She made a beeline for him.

"Look, get your stuff together man. He is happy and that was many years ago, please let it go," she pleaded with Tino.

"You are a fine one to talk. Look at you," he said trying to one up her.

"Oh, so you're going there, huh? Well, mine wants me, takes me out, fucks me on the regular, and loves me past this little friendship. My reality damn near mirrors my fantasy. Meanwhile, you struggling for attention from a person who doesn't even recognize your, what was it one night of passion? Oh, I mean that mistake. You have never had any interest in a man, why so curious? It's just the jail time and what you got used too. So swallow your fucking pride and let that shit ride. I does this," she said attempting to walk away, shaking her head very irritated.

"Look Chryssany, just because I didn't get my degree don't mean I'm gone sit here and let you play me. First of all my preference, is just that my own. And why the fuck should you even care?"

"Simple," she said, "I don't, but the shit you did at my house in MY bed was foul I got plenty other rooms, and on top of that, when did you become a homosexual?

So let me get this straight, so you and Alex cool, but I'm the problem, huh?"

"SO, you and the Shawn nigga cool, but I'm the mother fucking problem," he said stepping closer to her face.

"So what is it about boys that turn you on? I mean what do you think it is? I got pink, light brown, dark brown, black, and green dicks multiple sizes. Wanna try one?" she asked not backing down.

"Watch it, Syd," he said raising his voice

"What's going on in the corner," Damion said stepping in front of her.

"See what I mean?" she said winking, giggling, and pointing at Damion clearly protecting her and Alex not giving a fuck about his well-being.

"Yo, girl on some foul shit. You need to check her," Tino said attempting to push her forehead.

"Hold up. Calm down. I know what this is about. Just think. Some things happen on purpose and some things are evidently bad choices."

"Are you guys okay," Shawn said walking toward the disruption.

"Yea, they fine. That's between them, boo. Don't get involved. It's like a family arguing, just watch," Alex said trying to keep Shawn at a safe distance.

"Naw, family ain't got shit to do with this," Tino said aggressively.

"Should we leave?" Shawn asked.

"The fuck going on? Where the food at? Why y'all so close to her?" Mel said looking at Damion and Syd. "Why in hell you yelling about family?" she said pointing to Tino.

"Because I ain't no damn mistake," he said all too seriously.

"What the fuck? Boy, let that shit go," Mel said knowing exactly what he was talking about. "Hell, we all have."

"Well, since everybody got a fucking say so about my business. The shit I do, and who the fuck I do it with. Let me let y'all in on all the shit ya missing about each other." "Hmmm," he said, looking around where to start. "Okay, let's start with you D. You lead this bitch on," he said pointing to Chryssany, "Whenever the fuck yo ratchet trick get to acting even worse than she already act. And you know the bitch was pregnant when y'all started fucking with each other or so you thought, but hey you want that family right?"

"Tino, nigga, yo worthless nothing having ass, always with this bullshit. It's time to grow the fuck up.

This petty kid shit got old when you was 'in college'" he said laughing. "Fuck ya, stupid ass," Damion said walking past him toward the door.

"Oh, don't leave captain save a hoe, Syd. So it was rape? If yo ass don't drink, don't! But you let that nigga get you drunk and bone yo ass because his ratchet ass," pointing to the back of Damion' head, "ain't right. I understand getting over one and getting under the other, just never pegged you for the type," he said never losing eye contact with Chryssany.

"Is that what you did?" Chryssany asked walking past him.

"Bitch, you just mad I got it before you," he said as a matter-of-fact.

"I think I am going to be sick," Chryssany said running to her hall half-bath.

"Yeah, you got bruh over here all up in arms when it was yo horny ass just wanted the dick. Ain't you done learned by now? That big brain of yours obviously stuck on stupid. This the nigga you want," he said pointing over his shoulder, "but he don't want yo ass. You keep using these local jokers, irky jerks ass niggas as painkillers. Bitch, go buy you a dick, shit. You say you got plenty; use one!" he yelled down her hallway, turning to make eye contact with Alex. "You told me we were meant the shit was magic huh?"

Shawn chimed in, "Excuse me what the hell…"

"Oh, so everyone knows, but you? Well, I fucked yo man and he loved it. When I first got home, stayed here, right Syd?" he said as she reentered the dining room of her home. He said putting a finger on his chin as if he were thinking, "Yea, in your bedroom since you won't let me forget. Would have been better in any other room, huh?" he quoted Chryssany.

Rolling her eyes and shaking her head, she said, "Ugh you're so lame. That was before him, not while they were together you delusional twit," Chryssany said trying to fix it.

"No, it wasn't magic. It was a moment of weakness, not love. Pure lust, I love Shawn. What we did was a mistake," Alex said explaining to Shawn as much as Tino.

"You love him now, but then you said Shawn who? I can't forget, he called all night and day, but you sent him straight to voicemail. Hey, Shawn you remember a two a.m. message? 'He's the one you lost?' Yeah, I put him to bed," Tino said remembering his pettiness.

"You lying, cheating, bastard! You deserve this asshole as a friend," Shawn said storming out with tears filling his eyes.

"Babe no, it isn't like that. We weren't…" Alex began to explain.

Shawn slammed the door, started the car, and burnt rubber out of the driveway.

"Why are you doing this," Chryssany asked with tears in her eyes and hurt in her voice.

"Bitch, calm down," Tino said.

“Let’s see. Oh you..." He started in on Mel.

"Don’t come for me. I am all you got, and bitch you hurt my heart," she said releasing Chryssany from a hug. "So yo ass might want to tread lightly. Come for me, and I will end yo ol’ confused, misguided, rude, fucked up, felony having ass. Bitch, TRY IT!" Mel said, evening the playing field for him.

Seeing the seriousness in her tone, Tino backed down.

"Get the fuck out of my house, you trifling bastard. You are so ignorant; you can’t make anything work for you so you have to make everyone around you miserable. Leave now, you immature bomb! Don’t come back until you act right, with your scorn, love gone wrong, I need a man silly indecisive self!" Chryssany said more hurt and confused than anyone. "All ever did was look out for you and made sure you had something and somewhere to go, and this is how you repay me?" she said getting directly in his face. "I put men like you behind bars daily; I always thought there were good men who made bad decisions, look at Tino. No, you are a bad decision. Stay away," she said backing him out the kitchen entrance to her home.

Mel intervened. "Calm down boo. I got this" as she calmed Syd down. Get the fuck in the car, Tino. What the fuck were you thinking? You just alienated all of your closest friends. You will apologize to my girl so fucking help you."

"Look, I don't need you or your fucking lectures. My mother died a long time ago, and I been living ever since. I got me, trust," he said walking past the car.

"I hope you ain't planning to go to the sterling Faronia Square. Hell you bet not even enter the pepper tree. Get yo dumbass in before I expose you," Mel said pulling every card he thought he had.

"What the fuck? Who do you know? How do you know, and why do you know all my spots?" he said with a chaotic look on his face.

"Get the FUCK in the car, now!!!"

He got in with no more words.

Mel burnt rubber out of Syd's estates. "How could you do that to Shawn? He's just as much of a friend to you as I am, and plus NIGGA YOU AIN'T GAY! So what were you thinking?" Mel said with a little disgust in her voice.

"Mel, you remember my 'college days,'" Valentino said starting to explain.

"Yeah what that got to do with anything? Wrong is wrong," Mel said not moved by anything he was trying to say.

"Fuck it Mel," Valentino said looking out the passenger side window. "I thought I still had you, but I guess not. I know Syd is mad because this happened at her house and all the shit that keeps happening she already has a weak stomach. Damn I thought I at least had you, of all people."

"What are you talking about Valentino? You're talking in circles. Just spit it out. I'm trying to listen," Mel said impatiently.

"Well, just shut up and listen. When I was locked up I got a lot of knowledge on the homosexual lifestyle up close and personal, and I liked it too much and every night I found myself thinking about Alex, so when I wrote him just talking, he always wrote back and said some real shit. I thought it was fate, and I had to have him. Mel that night was supposed to change everything for us. He was supposed to choose me, not Shawn. I love Shawn like a brother, but Alex was supposed to choose me."

"You sound like Chryssany. Let that shit go, damn. It was fucking jailhouse love. He said what he said to help you pass time, not to make you fall in love. Hell, I wrote, put money on your books, sent pictures, magazines, shoes, all that shit. You wanna fuck me and fall in love too?" She asked, not taking her eyes off the road. "Let me call and check on, Syd and Alex. Hopefully, they aren't plotting to kill you. I know them.

Yo ass is grass, so shut the fuck up while I talk to them. Don’t even breathe loud."

He shook his head in agreement, finally realizing he had fucked up.

"Chryssany, are y’all okay?" Mel asked in a slow cautious tone.

"No, I have to call you back," Chryssany said hurriedly.

"What’s going on?" Mel asked panicking through the phone.

"I have to take Alex to the hospital. He is having an anxiety attack. He can’t catch his breath, can’t stop crying, and is clearly suicidal, uh, wait a minute hold on..."

"Hello?" Syd answered in a hurried voice.

"I can’t believe you kept that from me," Shawn started.

"Please let me call you back. Alex needs to go to the hospital," Chryssany begged, not needing any more of the drama.

"What? Why, what’s going on?" Shawn asked deeply concerned.

"He isn’t doing well, at all. I can’t help him here. I need to get him to the ER. I think it may be an anxiety attack or something, and he’s just not right. I can’t even communicate with him," Chryssany explained.

"No, he can't go to the ER. We have... look I am on my way. Take him to the guest room. Let him lie down, and just watch him. I'll be there in a moment. Don't let him by the window either," Shawn explained a little too familiar with how to take care of him.

"Okay," Syd said hanging up. She sat the phone down as it began to ring again. "Ugh, fuck me. Hello?"

"You're going to kill him, Tino is that what you wanted? You bitter ass, selfish, ugh. And we can't go back because you caused... gaddamn look what you did. I don't believe this shit," Mel said.

"Hello, Mel? Why is he still with you? Tell him I hope he's fucking happy low life," Syd said disconnecting the call. "Come on, boo. Let's get you lying down. It will be okay. Shawn is coming to take care of you, I promise," she said reassuring him

"He ain't coming girl. He said I had no more chances after that last incident. Bitch, he done walked in and some mo. Chile, this is the icing on the cake. He ain't coming," he said trying to catch his breathe

"Wait, what?" Syd said surprised. "I though two were in a good place and things have been good, at least since you both have become so successful. I know about when he first started traveling and you have your needs, but was this recent."

"Yes, he's always gone on some business trip or about to leave, or getting ready to leave, then he gets home and all so tired. I mean, I work, too, but I still want some love and affection," he cried. "I mean, hey baby, how was your day, would be great, or even I cooked for you honey. Not, the food is in the microwave not even looking over his computer screen to acknowledge my dissatisfied look, or disheveled nature after an affair that I kept under the radar. Yes, Shawn is the perfect gentleman, but that's only on vacation. I blame you," he said becoming enraged. "I should have got on that fucking plane, and this is your fucking fault." He rose off her bed, walking toward her. "You lonely miserable cunt. You did this to us," he said reaching for her throat.

"No, this is what you did," a deep familiar voice rang out.

"Thank you, Jesus," Chryssany cried out not looking back to see who had entered her home.

"We should have left," Alex said grabbing his chest. "I can't breathe."

Shawn rushed over to him. "Here are your meds. I just don't understand. We have been through so much. Why not tell me this? It was in the beginning of our love, where we both were unsure. I mean I had my transgressions and you had yours. We resolved them," Shawn said questioning their entire relationship.

"I know, but look at how close this was. I couldn't risk losing you," Alex explained fading into his slumber.

"No, we will get passed this," Shawn said resting Alex's head on the pillow.

"What's wrong with him? Why is he acting this way?" Chryssany said still standing in the corner.

"Alex has bi-polar Schizophrenia and because of the relaxed nature of our trip, I thought it best that he went off his meds, but the tension and drama caused him to have an episode. I shouldn't have left him, but I felt so foolish. Why wouldn't you tell me?" he asked, disappointed.

"It wasn't for me to tell," Syd motioned for him to come closer.

"He is out for a couple of hours. I gave him a tranquilizer and one of his regular meds."

"A tranquilizer?" Syd said with a skeptical look on her face.

"Nothing like that. It was prescribed. I am going to coax him into the car. I am so sorry this happened."

"Not, as sorry as I am," Syd said leaning against the doorframe. "Who else knows about his 'condition'?"

"No one and let's keep it that way, please. Not even your beloved Damion," Shawn said looking her directly in her eyes.

"Your secret is safe with me," Chryssany said backing out the room.

Syd ran down to her room, trying to escape what had just happened to her. She slammed the door and ran straight into the bathroom. She began violently vomiting and crying. She grabbed her phone to call Mel. She hit the number two and the phone began to ring.

"I will call you back. I am getting a damn ticket," Mel said into the phone as the hung up.

"License and registration," the officer said.

"What's the problem officer?" Mel asked in an irritated voice.

"Well, ma'am you were speeding," the officer began to explain.

"Um, no sir you are mistaken," Mel said attempting to reach under her seat.

"Mel, what the fuck, you doing?" Valentino asked.

"Ma'am keep your hands where I can see them," the officer said, placing his right hand on his weapon and the other on the window seal of Mel's vehicle.

"Damn, I thought it was black boys that got this shit," Mel said sucking her teeth and rolling her eyes.

"Step out of the vehicle, ma'am," the officer said taking a step back.

"Why, though?" Mel said folding her arms as she cocked her head to cut her eyes looking the officer in his face

"Fuck Mel, just do what he asked. You too fucking difficult. Damn," Valentino said in a stressed voice.

"Fuck you. Hell, this you fucking fault. I hope they Rodney King you ass," Mel said in a bitter but all too serious tone.

"Ma'am step out of the vehicle," the officer demanded. Mel finally got out and stepped to the side. "Sir, I need your ID and for you to also step out the vehicle."

"Fuck," Valentino said under his breathe.

"What was that?" the officer said.

Valentino just looked and sucked his teeth. Mel's phone rang

"What's up," Mel answered.

"I hope you dropped that nigga in the fucking river," Damion said.

"Um, unfortunately not," Mel responded.

"Ma'am, you need to get off the phone," the officer firmly requested.

"Look, man you searching my damn car, for speeding, so do your damn job, fuck!" Mel said trying to keep calm.

The officer radioed, "I need back up."

"Mel, what the hell is going on? What you do?" Damion yelled in the phone.

"Fuck, I'm about to go to jail," Mel said just as her phone hung up

"Ma'am, we found illegal drugs in your car," the officer explained just before reading her, her rights.

"What the … Ugh, I hate you," she said looking up at Valentino

Shamika

"So explain to me, how you go to jail for speeding, and drugs Mel? What were you thinking? How could you let this happen? In your line of work, you know better. If any of your charges were legit, you could kiss this life of yours goodbye. How could you be so stupid? I hope this night in here you figured out this shit ain't for you." Syd asked walking to her car from jail east. "Then, I have to hear about this from Damion. You know he can't keep a secret from his... whatever she is. She is going to have a field day with this. Say something Mel!"

"Where is my car? Where the fuck is Valentino? And thank you but, right now, please just shut the fuck up and get me to my shit," Mel responded, trying to mask her anger.

"Alright, but this isn't over. This conversation will be had and you will answer my questions," Syd explained as they approached her truck.

"Whatever just get me to my shit? Where is Valentino? We got a fucking problem?" Mel said snatching her door open.

"What's the problem? He didn't go to jail, you did!" Syd said tired of the drama and secrets.

"Look Mom, it was Valentino's dope, not mine. You know I know better than this. Shit, he is a fuck up. And filled with destruction and will fuck up anything he gets his hands on," Mel said rubbing the sweat off the palms of her hands onto her thighs.

"So, this is his fault, huh? But you were driving, right? Who was talking foolishness to the cops? You, huh? So again, how is this his fault? I mean, I would love to know that. I see you are upset, but damn Mel, accept some responsibility. You talked crap. You were speeding, and you let him in your car..."

"Syd, he's trying to destroy the little family I got. I was furious. I am livid now. How the fuck could he do this to me? Who called you anyway?" Mel asked remembering she didn't call anyone from jail.

"Valentino called. He was so upset and hurt that HE caused all this, but it wasn't him. Look at how we treated him. Look at how he was alienated, especially with the situation. He apologized to me, and we are having a dinner tomorrow night, for all of us. You will be there and you will not blame him. All your 'shit' is here," Syd said pulling into Mel's driveway. "And no worries. All the charges were dismissed. Nothing will show on your record. Please be more careful and think."

"I am going to carefully skin his ass, and think of a good place to dispose of his fucking body," Mel said jumping out of her friend's truck.

"But, Mel think," Syd said rolling her window down. "What the heck is that smell?" she asked as she started gagging. "Oh my goodness," she said seemingly making a new exit in her truck. "Open the door, please," she ran towards Mel's back door.

Valentino opened the door just as Syd approach and rushed past him and bee-lined to the bathroom.

"How dare you be here at my fucking house like we cool. Bitch, leave," Mel said walking towards Valentino.

"No, please let me explain, damn. It wasn't supposed to be like that. Why couldn't you just stay calm and take the fucking ticket?" Valentino asked trying to understand how they got in this situation.

"I was all you had, the only motherfucker willing to put up with all that bullshit, and look how you did me, and you fucking have the nerve to question me, boy? Bye," Mel said walking in the door to her house. "Just get whatever the fuck you got and leave. Bitch, ain't got time for a mafucka who ain't loyal."

"Fuck you man, ain't loyal? I had yo back since day fucking one even when you didn't know. What about the first time we met? Remember that? You were at Bellevue, all those females was about to jump you, and on top of that your leg was broken. Who had yo back and didn't know yo ass? Day 1, now let's fast forward to today, bitch. Yo smart mouth ass didn't pay attention to the fact that the amount of weed found wasn't a legitimate reason to arrest you. Then while you hating me, I had to tuck my dick and call because I know I fucked up, but you going to jail was on you. I know no one deserves that but this ain't my damn fault!"

"Let me explain something to you. I gives no fucks about you or your tucked dick. Seems like that's what you like anyway," Mel said sucking her teeth. "My fault? Bitch, if you would learn fucking tact, then this whole situation could have been avoided."

"Look, bitch, I helped you. I'm trying to thank you and apologize, and you want to be a bitch, fuck you ol' dumb ass ho," Tino said attempting to walk out the door.

"What the fuck you say to me, ho? Bitch! Aight I got yo ho," she said punching him in the back of the head.

"Mel, nooooooooo," Syd yelled running from the hall into the family room trying to get between them.

Valentino reached back into to what seemed like Mississippi in an attempt to slap Mel across the face. Unfortunately, Syd got there first and her ear popped and started ringing.

"Oh, bitch you done, done it," Mel quickly stepped on to her couch and jumped on to Tino's back, beating him in the head, with her legs wrapped around his waist.

"Hello, hello, D. I need your help," Syd yelled into her phone.

"My man is busy, bitch. Call yours!" With that, Shamika hung up

Enraged, Syd stands up, holding her ear, "Look, you two need to get this shit straight. Ugh, and you fucking hit me? Ugh, asshole. No, I am not taking him with me. Yes the fuck he is staying here. No, I don't give a fuck about either of you killing the other. Fuck both of y'all. Damn, my fucking ear. Ugh, fucking savages."

"Your phone is ringing, Syd," Mel said swiftly changing the subject.

Syd unknowing answered the phone, "Fuck this phone. Fuck y'all. Fuck Damion and his bitch. Fuck everybody. My damn ear is killing me."

"Maybe you shouldn't drive. We will drive you okay?" Valentino volunteered them both.

"Look b., you know what? We'll squash this shit later. He's right, girl. You ain't even hear your phone ring."

"Baby girl, I didn't mean to hit you. I tried to slap slob from this bitch. She hit me hard as hell. I probably got a knot. Damn," he said rubbing the back of his head.

"I hope so," Mel said smiling.

Syd just looked at them as if they were monkeys in the zoo.

"HELLO? HELLO?" a faint voice yelled from Syd's cell phone.

Mel picked it up. "Hello, who is this?"

"It's me. What the hell is going on over there, and who hit her?" he asked pissed to the maximum level.

"It was a misunderstanding. Look we about to take her home. You can meet her there to check, that is if you can get away from the old ball and chain," Mel said hanging up the phone not understanding why he and Shamika were included in Chrysanny's rant.

"Come on, look you drive my car. Hopefully, yo ass get locked up this time hell," Mel said rolling her eyes, taking Syd's keys out of her hand.

"What the... ugh. I need to lie down. Just get me home. Y'all got to do better."

They all got into their vehicles. Mel asked Syd, "What happened? Why did you include Damion in your little tantrum? What the fuck happened, Syd?"

"Why, is my life an open book, but I have to keep all y'all secrets? Damn, I want my secrets, too."

"Syd, you are the closest thing I have to a sister. Please just talk to me," Mel pleaded.

"I'm just saying please," Syd looked at her phone. She had three missed calls and suddenly an incoming one. DAMION. Syd began breaking down, the tears filled her face. With a cracked voice and broken words she said, “I must be broken, damn! This can't be it. Where the fuck is my happy ending? No matter how nice, how loyal, how hard I love, it’s never enough. Where is my Boaz? I just don't get it. I don't believe in karma because people can only do to you what you allow, but if I did, I would love to know what the fuck I have done to deserve this. I don't break hearts. I don't screw with people’s emotions, and I try to be one-hundred percent. Ugh, I'm broken mentally, emotionally, and relationally. All I can do is cry and shake my head. Damn, love fucking sucks!!!! I'm going to walk away from this before it breaks my heart. This cannot be it, and I honestly don't see how good people have to suffer. This trick is whorish. She can't be trusted. She does him any kind of way. She hurts him intentionally. She is having this baby just to pull his strings. Like, why do I have to suffer this shit? It's so unfair," she said through tears streaming down her face.

"Pull yourself together. Trouble don't last always. This is you being set up for your Boaz. You have to remove yourself from this situation. Look, I know it hurts right now, but you gotta see this is what’s best for you. She needs him, while you only want him. I know you love him. Hell, I even know how much, but you have to understand he don't love you like that. Being needed makes a relationship work, and a man that knows his woman needs him will be loyal to her. You are self-sufficient and a possible risk. You can leave at any time, and where does that leave him or y'all? It doesn't because you are again self-sufficient and only rely on you."

"That's that bull. What about me like, ugh," she said fighting the tears, trying to pull herself together. "You know what? Today is the day I remove myself from this crap. I am over being hurt and the victim. I can't believe Valentino hit me that hard," she said chuckling. "My dang ear is still ringing. I am glad you jumped on his back, man. I should have had my phone on record. Can you say 'World Star'?"

"You are a mess, honey. I don't know what to do with you. Are you seriously okay, though, like for real Syd?" Mel asked very concerned.

"I am fine," Syd reassured her.

"Well, I hope you stay that way," Mel said pulling into Syd's driveway, seeing Damion there waiting.

"Ugh, I don't believe this. I am going to put an end to this right now," Syd said as the car came to a stop.

"Please think before you speak. You're in a hurt place. Really think, is this what you want? Think hard, please," Mel pleaded.

"I got this," Syd said in an all cried-out tone.

"Well, before I get hit in the ear, I'm leaving. This is your secret to keep. I love you, okay, and thank you for having my back," Mel said leaning in to hug her far away friend.

"Love you too," Syd said getting out the car.

"What's up? What can I do for you, Syd?" asked Damion

"Well, we're out of here. Get yo punk ass over there. I'm driving my own shit," Mel said in a low tone

Syd waved her off.

"Look Syd, we need to talk. I'm sorry, but you know Mika and how she is. Whenever you need me, I will always make a way for you."

"Yea, unless she's there, right? I am not a priority. I'm just a piece of ass to you. This so called love you have for me is obviously just so you can feel better," she said unlocking her door and walking in. "I'm your pacifier, your pain killer, your fuck that makes me fall in love, but I'm not what you want. You want my affection, my closeness, my essence.... I can't do this anymore. It isn't working for me, this one sided love, NO."

"No, I have loved you since day one. I just got to get home right before we pick back up, you know? I mean, do you understand?"

"No, I don't because here I was thinking I am home, but I guess that's it, me thinking. Thank you for showing me the real you, and your priority list. See, it hurt at first to know I wasn't on it, but to add insult to injury ,you put her, a trick, a side piece gone wrong, before me,"

Syd said trying to keep her stern look on her face while facing him.

"Watch your mouth, Syd. I love her," Damion said defensively.

Syd's sternness began to break. "You love her?" she said through exasperated breathes. "You fucking love her? What about me? What about all the crap you said to me? Oh, fuck me, huh? Get the fuck out, you worthless asshole. I can't believe you were my savior. Stay the fuck out of my way! Tell your whore when you get home I said she can have you because I am officially done. Don't fucking come back," she said in a calm tone as she walked him to the door. "Stay away," she said as she pushed him out.

"Syd, let's talk about this," Damion said not understanding how they got to this point.

"Go talk to your whore. When she breaks your heart again, find a new Mrs. Fix It. I fucking quit, bum," Syd said slamming her front door. She turned away walking towards her kitchen. "Where's that wine? I can't take this mess. I give up. Where is my phone?" she said looking over her dark marbled counters. "Ah, cordless."

"Syd, let me in. We aren't done. Talk to me," Damion said trying one last time.

Syd looked through her door and shook her head while pointing to the phone mouthing, "I'm on the line."

"Hey, you what are you up to? I miss you babe. Come see me maybe?" Syd said calling one of her painkillers.

Damion rubbed his head, dropped his head, bounced down her steps, hopped into his truck, and slowly drove off. "Damn, I can’t believe this. I lost her."

Syd went into her bedroom to get her things out preparing for an evening all about her. She turned on her surround sound, putting K. Michelle on repeat, "I just wanna fuck, and it don’t make me no slut." On repeat, she began to sing aloud as she manicured and cleaned up any hair out of place, pulled her hair up in a messy bun, so when the fun started, she could just pull it down. She found a skimpy lace nighty where her perky breast were half hidden and half shown, and her nipples peaked through the lace. She slipped on a pair of her black spiked eight-inch red bottoms. "Tonight anything goes," she said as she poured the last bit of wine. She straightened up her room and the journey to the room. She went into her wine stash and got another bottle and two glasses. She decided to make some shrimp and chicken alfredo, with sundried tomatoes, basil, mushrooms, and a side of garlic bread. Something light and quick that wouldn't weigh her down before she got what she needed to feel all better. Her doorbell rang. She smiled and walked seductively to her door. Not looking up, with a seductive smile, she said, "I have been waiting for you."

"Really? I thought you didn't want to speak to me again," Damion said.

"Ugh!" Frustrated Syd said, "What do you want? I am expecting company any minute!"

"So you get dressed up, have the house smelling good. You even cooked for the nigga, Really, Syd? You are mine. No one gets this but me. Why are you doing this to us?" he asked.

"There is no us, and I am seriously having company. Please leave," she asked disregarding everything he said.

"No, not until we come to a resolution. I need to know where we stand. If I could have my cake and ice cream I would, but I have responsibilities at home," Damion said justifying how Shamika talked to her.

"You sure didn't have a problem eating my cake and ice cream recently. You are so pathetic. She yanks, you go running. She doesn't even genuinely love you like I do, but you don't love me like I love you. So I guess that's just the way love goes, huh?" Syd said slowly walking down the corridor into her bedroom.

"How exactly do you love me? That's what I need to know, but even if you do, how do you expect me to choose you? She's carrying my son. You can't be that selfish, not you Syd," he said walking behind her trying to make eye contact.

"Seriously, you want me to compete with a baby? Like seriously? What about me and all the crap you promised? How is it one day, it is your son, then the next you're recounting the minutes, hours, and seconds to backtrack to make sure there is a possibility? Selfish, I was yours and you were mine, until we fall out and a month later she moves in. She's pregnant, and y'all in love. Please!" Syd said rolling her eyes, pulling her robe over her nighty. "Let me explain this to you. You and I have had many different moments, but obviously our moments have passed. Although, in my heart and mind you were my ending, and I yours, inside you I was a place holder until Miss Ratchet walks up and 'needs' you again. Just leave," she said waving him off.

"So what? You just about to give MY shit away? You just wanna fuck, huh?" he said turning and slapping her stereo, abruptly interrupting K. Michelle.

"What the heck is wrong with you? YOUR shit is at YOUR home. This is all me," she said rubbing her hands up and down her body.

"Na, you gave me you, and I never gave you back. Look, I don't know what you got going on in that beautiful brain of yours, but I am and will forever be yours. No one can take the place of you in my heart. In my life, you have been my friend forever," he said walking up, grabbing her shoulders, looking her directly in her eyes. "And not just a friend, but a very best friend. You keep my secrets, you have my back, and you see the good in me when I can't. Hell, you make me a better man. I would be a fool to let you leave or to be without you. I can't let you feel this way and not do anything about it. You have been my Queen since day one. You showed me friendship, love, tested my loyalty, yet here we are," he said caressing her cheeks, wiping the tears away. "Queen, you are my best friend. We have a no-matter-what type of love, meaning," he said putting his lips on hers to make her lips say it with his, "no matter what, you and I are solid."

Pulling away, she said, "Please, if this is love, I never want it; I am your side chic to every Jane, Jill, and Joanna. That doesn't feel good to know that, and don't call me Queen," she said allowing the tears to flow freely. I can't continue to be your back up plan. I want something building up to something, not just a right now something."

"I am leading up to something. You think I'm going to marry her? NO, I am not, but if that is my son I have to be a man and do right," he said wrapping her in his arms. "I am telling you, you are it for me. No one else, but you," he continued, kissing away her tears. "Please don't shut me out. Please just understand."

Syd stood completely still with tears in her eyes, her arms straight down at her sides, looking him square in the eyes. "So if this is your kid, where does that leave us? How can you honestly expect me to be okay and I sleep alone every night while the man I thought to be my soul mate has another woman wrapped in his arms, holding her, protecting her, and making her feel safe? "

"I don't hold her at night, Queen. It doesn't feel right. I only hold you because I have been cuddling with you since our love affair began, and you are my everything. This just happened. I need you girl. I need your number to show up in my phone. I need you to call me when things aren't so great. I need to answer and hear the frustration in your voice just to ask what's wrong. I need you to call me and tell me the funny things that happen to you sporadically, so I can share those moments. I need you to need m., I need to know you are okay. I need you to be there when things aren't going so well, or when I can get an idea for my next project. I need you to be my secret keeper, my conscious, my guiding light when I can't make a decision. Please just give me some time before you do this. Whoever he is, he doesn't deserve a chance at my prize."

"Your prize?" Sydsaid trying to remove herself from his embrace.

Damion held tighter. "No, you belong to me. Remember the night I held you close and made passionate love to you, slow and deep, and the tears fell down your cheeks? I whispered in your ear, 'You belong to me.' I meant every word." He kissed her forehead. "Believe me please," he begged.

"I can't. I mean, how can I?" she started to stammer.

"Shhhhh," he whispered as he kissed her lips lovingly. "I am here and will be forever and a day. Remember?" he said revealing here infinity tattoo that matched his. She smiled a weary smile, and looked down as her tears hit the floor. She shook her head as no words could escape her lips. He lifted her chin with his pointer finger. "Trust me," he said as he slid her robe over her shoulders, guided it down her back, kneeled in front of her and gently placed it on the floor. He began to touch her body through the lace. She moaned aloud. He gripped her thighs. Raising her right thigh to his lips, saying to her with kisses through every word, "Be mine. Our love is bigger than you and I. You belong to me." Moving up to her almost dripping throbbing spot, massaging it with his tongue, "Is it mine?" he asked her, not really expecting a response. She moaned, allowing the frustration, anger, and hurt to drip from her body as he sucked them out through her pounding clitoris. She gave into him, as she always did. He lifted her body on to his shoulders as he devoured her. She gripped massaged his scalp with her fingertips. Her release began as her descent to her plush, white carpet. He laid her on her back, still wanting to taste her love.

She begin begging, "Please, give me yourself," she moaned as her body began to tense. Her eyes filled with tears as her mind began to catch up with what was happening. "Stop. STOP, Damion, please this isn't right!" Her doorbell rang.

"Dang, he's here. Why can't I just have a little bit of my own happiness?" she said standing. "Yes I love you, and yeah, I may be weak for you, but I am not yours. You made that decision." Her doorbell rang again. "Please just let me have myself back. Keep the love," she said, looking down at the door. "I can make more. Just go be with your woman. I got this."

"Who is this dude you so concerned with? You are MINE, and she is the place holder," he started to explain.

"D, please," she said wanting to get to the door.

"NO, no, you don't get yourself back, and I ain't going nowhere," he said standing his ground.

"NO, Damion. Why please, just please," she said exasperated. "I can't breathe." She clutched her chest. "I don't believe you. Why?" she said in thick, heavy breathes with each word. She attempted to look in his eyes, saying, "This can't be love." She searched his eyes in an attempt to see his soul. The room began to spin. "D, what did you do me?" Tears flowed down her face. "Help me," she whispered.

As her body went limp, he caught her. "Syd, baby? Baby girl, what's wrong with you?" He laid her gently on the floor, ran to the door wanting to know who was so important that she would replace him. Only the lights shown out as the car left the driveway. "Fuck, what to do? And she needs help" he spoke aloud in a whisper. "Fuck," and his mind began to race. "I need her." He grabbed the phone and dialed 9-1. "No, she wouldn't want to be seen like this, and how would I explain this to Shamika?" He dialed again. "Hello, Mel?"

"Who is this, D? What's up? So I guess y'all made up, huh?" she said figuring they must have made up for him to be calling from Syd's phone.

"No, get here now. Come alone. She isn't doing well. She needs help," he said going back to Syd's seemingly lifeless body. "I don't know what to do." He heard Mel's car start.

"What did you do to her? I will murder you and that bitch if she is hurt, I promise you!" she said hanging up.

He scrambled around looking for something else to put on her body. He went to his clothes drawer in her room and grabbed a T-shirt, returned to her side, lifted her from the floor. "SYD," he yelled, "Wake up, please. Syd, please, I need you to be okay. Wake the fuck up!" he yelled as the tears of sadness, confusion, love hurt, pain, and all his good intentions, flowed down his face.

"WHAT THE FUCK DID YOU DO TO HER," Mel yelled as she pulled him off Syd's bed.

"I didn't. She was talking to me. I thought we were okay, then her doorbell rang. She switched on me. She put me out. She act like she didn't want me," he said in a far away, voice. "Who the fuck was that?" he said no longer talking to Mel.

"GET THE FUCK OUT!" Mel scream. "Syd, what happened? What did he do to you?" she said checking her pulse, putting her face close to Syd's to feel her breathe. "She's barely breathing," Mel said grabbing her friend's pajamas and sliding them on. "Please tell me you called 9-1-1," she said attempting to get her friend off the bed and closer to the door to go get help.

"I couldn't. How can I or would I explain this to Shamika? You know my..." he said justifying letting their friend seemingly die.

"You know what? fuck you and that bitch! Go home, you piss poor excuse of a man, you pathetic low life, scum asshole," she said struggling to get Syd out of the house.

"Let me help I am not any of that you know that, please. Not you, too. Just let me explain. Let me help," he said picking Syd up, carrying her to Mel's car and gently placing her inside.

"Go home you bum. Haven't you helped enough? If anything is wrong, seriously, I am going to kill you with my bare hands," she said slamming her car door, peeling out of the driveway.

"Damn, damn, damn." He got in his car, grabbed his phone and saw that he had 35 missed calls from home, WIFEY Cell, WIFEY home, Office…. He saw 23 new voicemails. "Shit, this can't be happening." He sat back, put his head back on his headrest as he saw lights pull into Syd's drive. He just sat there thinking *what just happened*?

A hard bang, bang, bang, on his window. "Why can't you answer your fucking phone? I figured you were her at this bitch's house." Oh, but best believe I ain't going. Where the fuck is she?" Shamika screamed at his window.

He raised his head slowly looking out the window thinking, "Damn, I chose wrong. This can't be happening."

"You hear me, motherfucker? I got yo seed, and you wanna play me? Oh, bitch no one plays Shamika," she said still banging on his window.

He started his car, cracked his window, and in a calm tone he said to her, "Go home and I will be there. NOW!" he growled at her.

Surprised, she stepped back and said, "Okay."

Damion dialed Mel, "Please pick up, please."

"Hey, you got me. Leave a message," Mel's voice said.

He dropped his phone as the tears again fell; he drove as if he were racing, but with no clear destination in mind. He revisited his recent moments in his mind. "Let me have myself back. No!" he growled, banging his fist on the steering wheel. "I need you, Noooo!" he yelled, trying to recompose himself.

"Baby, what's wrong?" She began to beat on the window again, weeping for him.

He sat up, realizing, "Damn I chose her again." The tears wouldn't stop. He calmly got out the car walked passed Mika and into their home. He had driven there without even realizing that was where he was going.

"Baby, talk to me. What the fuck happened?" she asked. "Where were you? Talk to me. God damn it," she began to cry.

He saw the panicked look on her face, the same look he saw in Syd's before she passed out. *Not again*, he thought. *I can't lose her, too*. "Baby, calm down. I'm alright. Just got some things going on."

"Why were you over there?" she asked, looking him in his eyes with hurt and anguish on her face.

"I went to talk with a friend as I always do when I can't come to a resolve, but she wasn't there," he lied to ease her mind.

"Well, why you ain't answer the phone? Why can't you talk to me? Why you always gotta go to her? I'm right here. Use me. I'm yours. I'm here for you." Shamika poured her soul to him.

"This was about business, babe. You wouldn't understand the parameters of that conversation," he said settling back into his normal self.

"So what, you going broke or something?" she asked with a clear mind and heart.

He chuckled and sucked his teeth. "No your routine isn't in jeopardy."

"Where you going?" she asked as he walked away from her.

"Shower. You coming?" he said not looking back.

"Yes, Daddy," she smiled walking up the steps.

His phone rang in his pocket. It was Mel. "Hold up. I got to take this."

"Where you at? You ain't even gone check on her? You are a total piece of shit, asshole," Mel whispered in the phone.

"What's going on? How is she?" he asked as he entered the bathroom closing and locking the door.

"Don't know yet, but you don't give a fuck so why ask?" she said calmly still wanting someone to talk to, needing an emotional connection

"I do. Please, if you know anything, tell me," he begged. "Is this my fault, what can I do?"

"Stay away. Stay at home. Play house. Leave her alone," Mel said disconnecting the line.

His tears again began to flow. "This shit can't be real. Damn, I messed up." He got in the shower and let the pain and disappointment go down the drain with the water.

"Babe, I'm ready," Shamika knocked on the door.

"Not now. I'll be out in a second," he growled through the water and tears.

"Okay, Papi," she said walking into their guestroom, changing into her pink lace, crotch-less teddy and her 10 inch clear healed platform shoes, pulling her curly hair down to drape her shoulders down to just before her erect nipples. She lay on the bed on her side with her back to the door to camouflage her pregnant belly.

Damion walked in not really in the mood. "Baby what are you doing?" he asked, looking at her body and shoes, comparing her to Syd, her body her classy style, and expensive taste.

She peeked over her shoulder. "You don't have to do anything. Let me, please," she said in an erotic voice. "Let me relieve the stress. Let me relax you, Daddy," she said crawling across the bed, reaching for his arm, walking her hands up his body. She began kissing his lips, tracing the bottom one with her tongue then the top, then tracing the center where they meet. Parting his lips, their tongues met. She gently sucked his tongue as he slowly inserted his tongue in and out. She placed kisses down to his neck to kiss and lick on his neck, while nibbling in between his neck and jawline. Still going down, she kissed his chest, while writing her name on it with her tongue. Reaching his nipples, she teased them on her decent down to his belly button where she kissed it deep as if she were back at his lips. Still journeying down, she kissed the tip just enough to get a sample, while caressing his perineum. She meticulously sucked his balls, then licked up his shaft as if it were her favorite ice cream, not wanting to waist a drop. At the tip she gently circled the rim just before inserting him into her throat where she tried to put it all in her mouth, coming up only to slurp the tip and back down, enjoying every inch, as she began her expedition back up, She revisited his navel with a supple simple peck, back up to his chest, Just looking at it made her pearl drip with just a thought. She circled his nipples with her tongue, just before drawing it into her mouth with a tender pop between her lips as his nipple escaped, then the other, continuing to his neck where she again nibble and sucked as if it were her last bit of oxygen. She sat back as he lied there in enjoyment. She breathed his dick into her warm, wet wanting body. She placed his hands on her hips to balance as she rode slowly, as the juices flowed out onto his pelvis. She unmounted him to deep throat his dick because she couldn't resist tasting her juices mixing with his as he exploded in her mouth.

She lifted her head, attempting to make eye contact with him, noticing the faraway look on his fac., "What's wrong with you? You didn't like it?" she said standing.

"Na, it was good. Just still got a lot on my mind," he said shifting his weight to lift his upper body onto his elbow.

She huffed as she stood folding her arms. "This about that bitch, huh? You weren't over there talking bout no business. What the fuck is going on?"

Her phone began to ring. "TERRANCE <3," it said. Damion asked in a calm tone, "So who is Terrance?"

She froze. "What you talking about? Give me my phone," she said trying to snatch it from his hands.

He dropped it on the bed, "And why does he have a heart by his name?"

She picked it up and ran into the bathroom.

He grinned. "That's messed up. I'm severing ties trying to make us okay and look at what you got going, damn," he said looking around for his phone.

"You want to make us okay? Coming in here trying to be the hero, but this ain't no movie, fairy tale, or shit like that. I am real, man, this baby is real. The head you got didn't it feel real? The nut I swallowed surely tasted real enough for me to taste the pineapple juice you been on regime drinking. Why the fuck do you always pick the most fucked up times to say shit to me? You ask the dumbest questions and then have the nerve to expect a response," Shamika said yelling from the bathroom, rolling her neck while looking in the mirror and brushing her teeth.

"What was fucked up? I asked who the fuck is Terrance. Hell, you should be glad, that I am only asking, and not asking yo ass to leave," Damion said unmoved picking up his phone texting

Syd: "R U OK? R U STILL AT THE ER? I'M OMW."

"Why you got to threatened me, though? One day I am gone leave this mafucka never come back. You gone miss this hot sweet ass, and you can say goodbye to this baby," she said threatening him back.

"Please, you can't take care of yourself. I can trust you can't take care of a baby alone. Yeah I know you think that 'street crap' is where it's at, but I know. I work hard every day to make this lavish life work for you, and I didn't get here investing and trying to make all the best moves to allow you to keep me from my child. As a matter of fact, shit you should watch your mouth, because you will be back on the streets childless. Keep talking. I will put yo ass back on those damn streets you fucking love so much!"

"Don't you threaten me and my baby. This kid is mine", she said running in the room pouncing on the bed. "You hear me? I did this. He is mine," she said beating him in the chest.

"WHAT THE FUCK IS WRONG WITH YOU?" Damion shouted, pushing her off him watching her body hit the floor. He grabbed a pair of jogging pants, and a V neck white T and put them on along with his Nike shocks

"Oh, you done did it. You going to jail now; you put your hands on me. Oh, they coming for yo ass. Where the phone? You fucking put your hands on me. Yo ass gone get it. You gone get it," she yelled, crawling across the floor.

"Trick, you crazy," he said lifting himself from the bed examining the marks she had placed on his neck and chest. "I got the best attorney in tow, and bruises. You got a record, are an ex-offender, and you have cried wolf before. Furthermore, we in Memphis. If I ride, we both ride. You press charges, so will I. You want to have my child in jail so be it, but I will be out before you, and I will take custody of him. So keep playing pussy and watch you gone get fucked, best believe that," he said smiling that smile with his dimples showing.

"Where that come from," she asked. "What you doing? Where you going? Damion answer my fucking questions. What you doing? Hello?????"

"Don't worry about it," Damion said dashing down the steps dialing Mel

"You got me. Leave a message."

"Answer the damn phone!"

"Who you calling? Is it the Syd bitch? Keep trying me, and I'm gone fuck her up," Shamika said threatening Syd as her belly pushed him in the back.

Damion swiftly turned around, wrapped his right hand around her neck, pulling her face passed his, whispering in her ear, "Keep being ignorant. I will take you back to where I got you from, so back down, and don't ever threaten her again," He slowly pushed her back, making eye contact, not releasing her neck. "Do I make myself clear?"

"Yes, yes, I got it. I'm sorry," she said backing down, seeing the seriousness in his face.

"Good," he said removing his hand, turning and walking out the door.

"Where you going, baby?" she asked under her breathe, watching him enter his car and drive away.

He rolled his window down and yelled, "Don't wait up," and drove away.

"Where are they? Why won't they answer? I know what," he thought. He drove until he reached Syd's home. "*She has to come back.*" He went in his trunk to search for the key she gave him. "Where is it, where is it?" He reached under his tire. "Yep, here it is."

The Dinner

"Mel," Syd said finally waking up in the hospital, "What happened? Where are we? Why are we here?"

"Well, first calm down. Secondly, that slap you got was a bit more serious, and when you were upset and your blood pressure rose, the effects took hold and you passed out," Mel explained to her.

"Where is Damion?" Syd sat up looking around.

"He went home," Mel said getting up, removing her jacket from the front of her body." Humph, guess he has other pressing matter to attend to."

"Awesome, has Terri called me yet?" Syd said switching to business.

"No, honey, your phone was left at home. We, well I, was worried and didn't want to take the time. Wanted to be sure you were okay," Mel explained standing over the bed.

"Oh okay," she said in a faraway tone. "Well, why are we still here, I feel fine. Do they have my insurance information?" Syd asked removing her feet and legs from under her hospital blankets.

"Yes, they do, but what you trying to do?" Mel asked folding her arms.

"Where are my shoes? We're leaving?" Syd said in a nonchalant tone standing.

"No, we are not," Mel said standing her ground." Get back in bed."

"I will call a driver. They have my card on file. I am ready to go home," Syd said in a stern voice, looking around for the phone.

"Okay, Miss Thing, since you ready let's go. Here are some hospital socks," Mel said handing her the beige socks with the white slip resistant bottom. "I'm not going to argue with you on this, so let's go. Whatever you don't know, I guess they will call you. And, if you are dying, you will be home dying alone," she said looking into Syd's eyes.

"Well, with the way I feel right now I will go in my sleep, so I probably won't know," Syd said standing putting the socks on. "So where did you park?" Syd asked walking out hospital room the door.

"Right this way," Mel said in a huff, leading her down the hall passed the discharge desk. There was a brief silence while they both pondered the situation. "You know what, I don't understand you sometimes, but you got this," Mel said in an aggravated tone as they reached the exit. "Stay here I'm going to get the car."

"K, thanks," Syd said in a chipper voice. As she stood there, she couldn't help but think about her visitor and what happened. Her mind raced, trying to recollect the night. The doorbell rang, and rang, and then it didn't. *So maybe, I don't know*, she thought trying to gather herself as she saw Mel's car round the corner. She began to smile as Mel pulled to the door. "Thanks," she said. "I know you don't always understand, but trust me I do know what I'm doing," she said as she got into the car.

"Yeah, hear you, but you the only sister I got and I have to be sure you okay," Mel said as she pulled out of the parking lot. "So you might think you got this, but I have to make sure. This is some serious shit and you treating like you coughed or had a sore throat."

"Oh, Mel, you worry too much," Syd said resting her head on the headrest, hearing a vibration.

"Aight keep laying back like that. Fall asleep if you want to. Yo ass gone wake thinking you in the Twilight Zone 'cause you gone be back at the hospital tied the fuck down, "Mel said never taking her eyes off the road.

"I expect to wake up at home, because that's what I asked you to do," Syd said reclining the seat.

"I hear ya," Mel said in an "I don't give a fuck" voice.

Syd combed her mind trying to fill in the details of the night, before. *I cleaned, I cooked, I got cute, Damion... there it is again, that vibration.* "Where is Damion?" Syd said aloud.

"How the hell should I know," Mel responded with an annoyed look on her face.

"Well, how did you know to come over?" The buzzing began again. "What is that?" Syd said in a louder than usual voice.

"I don't hear anything. Maybe you should have stayed at the hospital," Mel said side-eyeing her.

"Or, maybe it's your phone. Is it Valentino? Did you guys come to terms? You didn't do anything crazy did you? He's family, too, Mel. What's going on?" Syd said as all bad things flooded her mind

"Dayum, you need a Valium. Calm down! We squashed our beef; he knows to stay in his place. Hell, you should know. He told you about the dinner before he told me." Mel explained about Valentino carefully leaving out the phone that was currently ringing.

"Yes, I did, but that was before all of this, and y'all and this drama… You know what never mind," she said looking out the window seeing she had made it home. "Thank you Mel," she said opening the door before the car was at a complete stop.

"Aight, yo ass gone be back in the hospital for a broken leg. Slow down. We here now," Mel said not putting the car in park.

"I know, now I can shower and put on any shoes I like," Syd closing the door.

"Yeah, any shoes," Mel said driving out the other side of Syd's drive.

Chryssany walked up to her door realizing; NO SHOES, NO PHONE, and NO KEY. She began to sprint down the drive yelling and waving her hands indistinctly, "MEL, MEEEELLLLLL, MEL!" only taillights. *Man, this can't be happening* she thought as she walked back up the drive and onto her backporch where she plopped down, putting her head in her hands, then running her finger tips through her hair, to think and remove it from her face.

"Chryssany, baby girl what's wrong?" he asked

Almost jumping out of her rocker she asked, "Where did you come from, and where is your car?" she asked trying to control the mini heart attack she had just encountered.

"I was in the house. Where is Mel? Why didn't she see you in the house?" he asked helping her into the house

"She has a ton of stuff on her mind, and has to deal with her own personal stuff," she said being elusive and truthful.

"But," he said in a confused tone, "why wouldn't she see you in, ugh? I just sometimes don't understand…"

"You cleaned up my kitchen? And washed my clothes? Wow, how long have you been here?" Syd asked looking at Damion. "Why would you do this?

What about Shamika and her needing you? Why would you do this?" Her head began to spin and she started to get confused.

"No, baby girl, no please calm down," he said wrapping her in his arms. "Shhhhhhh," he said trying to calm her spirit. He rocked her back and forth and caressed her spine up and down slowly. "Calm down." He lifted her body and walked her into the bedroom, passed the bed and into her bathroom. "Syd," he said in a calm whisper, "I ran a bath for you with the bubbles just like you like it."

Syd's, eyes were glossy with a faraway look.

"Syd, don't do this again," he said gently placing her on her heated floor. He removed her clothes slowly, praying, "Not again, please God, not again. I need this lady to be okay."

"What are you doing? No stop," she said in a low, slow, quiet voice.

"Syd, baby please, it's me," D said with tears in his eyes. "I love you, please. I'm here for you, for your heart, baby please," he said trying to see her in her distant eyes.

"Damion, Damion?" Syd questioned as she was coming back.

He lifted her and placed her in the tub. "I'm here. Are you okay?"

"No, no, no, what happened? This can't be happening," Syd's tears began to flow. She began to rock and cry uncontrollably.

"What's going on? Talk to me, I'm here. Please tell me," Damion said, tears streaming down his face into her bath and mixing with the warm water.

"When I was a girl, I used to have really bad seizures, so much so that my dad tried to never get me upset. Then, as I got older I had to take on the attitude that I really didn't care for anyone or anything because it was literally bad for my health. And now they are back I don't know what triggered it, but no, I can't deal," she said again as her tears restarted.

"Look, Syd, I'm here. Talk to me," Damion pleaded as he kneeled on the pedestal beside her tub.

"Yea, you are, right now, so I can't depend on you. That phone rings and out you go. You know what, right now, how I feel?" she said becoming angrier and angrier as the seconds passed. She stretched her legs out sat straight up, with tears in her eyes. "We have been at this for years and I keep my little black book on standby, but whenever I pull that card you always stop me, which make any other relationship become just sex and I become the painkiller. Therefore I have to get the random booty calls that I hate, and all the wretchedness," her blood began to boil as she spoke through gritted teeth. "Sometimes it feels like I got the short end of a long fucking stick. I'm supposed to jump when a mafucka say and guess how high and if it ain't high enough, I'm selfish, and don't give a fuck about nobody but myself. But I'm supposed to be content with what's given. Damn, I don't deserve shit? Or maybe I just like seconds or leftovers or something. Man, sometimes I swear people real live don't fuck with me. They just deal with me for whatever they can get from me. Shit crazy as hell man, man," she said shaking her head hardening her heart to life, or trying to.

"Syd, what are you saying? Who are you? Where is this coming from? What about me? What about your friends?" Damion asked trying to talk to the person he thought he knew.

"To be honest, FUCK EVERYBODY," Syd said sinking into the tub, hair and all.

Damion sat back, trying to recollect the moments that just passed, looking over the water wondering if she would ever come back.

Syd reappeared, "Hey," she said looking at the dismay on Damion' face. "No worries, just have to hit the reset button. When you allow the wrong people in, it drains you, but when you allow them in and they stay it can destroy you. I just have to clear my head and heart, from the hurt and pain, and reorganize my relationships."

"But, you are perfect the way you are. You don't need to change. What about me and us?" he said still in shock of the person he just met.

"You are one of my main problems. I hold you on a pedestal, and I'm the gum on the bottom of your shoes." Syd brushed her hair out of her face. "I mean, our times are fun, but Shamika calls and there I am pushed to the side, no matter how badly she treats you or no matter how she defames your name. I'm your cheerleader and she's your queen. Can you understand how it feels to have to hear about your quarrels, and how bad she is towards you? But, I sing your praises and blindly support you because I see the man not just his potential, the heart, the actual dream realized. Meanwhile, she only sees the thug she met, that would go upside anybody head, including hers, for looking at him wrong. But, I see the man with limitless possibilities, who doesn't allow anything to stand in his way, but, "she paused, "Shamika. So yeah, we needs to cool it. We aren't equal. To you I am a pretty face, with a nice ass, that gets stupid wet, and listens when your world seems to be not so right. But, if I need you at the same time she does, I lose. I'm tired of losing. I choose me, not you because if I keep choosing you over me, I will lose myself, and I love me too much to allow that to come to pass." Damion, looked up with no words, with tear-filled eyes, shook his head side to side slowly as he began to mouth the word "NO." "I have to be selfish," Syd said as her tears would no longer fall. "I'm sorry," she said as she lay back in the tub. Damion simply stood and walked out of what she thought was her life. Syd bathed slowly as she washed all the bad, negative energy away. She stood to turn on her shower, to watch as all the crap she had just spoken went down the drain. She reached out for her towel and was surprised it reached back for her. "What is going on?" she said aloud.

"I want my chance to speak. I need you to understand my point of view," Damion said in his soft soothing voice.

"Ugh, D I got it. I understand. She's the mother of your child. She needs you, blah, blah, blah. I know," Syd said becoming agitated with the conversation.

"Yes, all that may be true, but what about you? Since day one I knew you were special. We didn't just have a physical connection. It was like telepathy. You were and are in my mind, my thoughts, and my heart. I can't go too long without you. It just ain't right."

"Look D, I don't need a cheerleader. I work hard to be okay by myself and when my Boaz does come along, I will be prepared without being mentally, spiritually, or emotionally broken. Thank you for the consideration, but I will pass," she said stepping out of the tub, grabbing her towel, and wrapping it around her.

"Syd how can you say that? Where is this coming from," he said walking behind her out of her bathroom.

"A very hurt and misunderstood place," she said as she entered her bedroom, plopping down on the bed. "See, I always seem to be the one getting hurt, but I always have to be the one with the smile on my face, and seemingly okay. Well I am not always as okay as I seem. What about those long lonely cold nights, where I sleep alone and pray that I get a goodnight text because you're over there with your other half?"

"Syd, that's not fair," Damion said not understanding why she wouldn't just bounce back like usual. "Syd are you listening to yourself? Why would you? How could you think something like that?"

"Your phone is ringing," she said listening to the vibrations loud and clear.

"Hold up. We're not done," he said putting one finger up. "Hello, what? What are you talking about? She did huh? Okay. I'll be there. You just get out stuff ready," he said hanging up. "So, you told Mel to invite Shamika to Tino's dinner, huh? Aight fine Syd, that's how you want it? Fine by me!" Damion walked over to her bed where she was applying generous amounts of lotion. He bent down and kissed her forehead. "I love you girl. Maybe one day you will believe that."

"Oh, I know you love me, just not in love with me," she said watching him walk out of her room.

"See, there you go again. Leaving me alone, don't be surprised when I'm not who you expect next time," she said just before she heard the front door close. She leaned back across her bed then rolled over and crawled under her light blue and chocolate duvet. Just as she got comfortable, her phone rang. "Ugh," she said leaning over and picking up the phone. "Yes?"

"Ugh, how are you feeling, Miss Rudeness?" Mel asked.

"I'm feeling well. How are you feeling Misses Snippy?" Syd asked

"I'm me. So you know you only have a few more hours. The dinner is tonight. Tino said don't be late. As a matter of fact, be early. Shamika said her and Damion will be there. Alex and Shawn have agreed to come, stay, and eat."

"Um, okay. Do I have time for a quick nap? I really need to recharge and clear my mind," Syd said in an exhausted voice.

"Yeah, but don't sleep too long. I'd hate for the Twilight Zone to come get ya," Mel said snickering into the phone.

"Honey, I know who would have put me there," Syd said taking the phone from her ear, looking at it as if it were a miniature Mel.

"Um, okay so you were my last call so make sure you're on time," Mel said in a whine.

"Yeah, whenever I'm on time I end up being the only one there, so can you guys please be on time at 5:00, right?" Syd asked relaxing back into her comfortable position.

"Yes," Mel said sharply.

"Okay, great see you then," Syd said hanging up her cordless phone and tossing it anywhere in the bed. "Okay, so sleep here I come."

Syd fell fast asleep. Her mind took her back to the previous night when her visitor came to her door. She tried to get into his mind. What did he see? What could he see? He stood there a little while as he rang the bell again. He just stood there with no apparent need, reason, or knowledge of why he was invited. There he stood, Syd thought wanting to reach out to him, grab his hand, call his name or in the least to say thank you for showing up. But, she couldn't do it. She couldn't let him see her, not knowing what's going on inside that house. She watched him calmly walk back to his car and drive away. Sadness came over her. *Why can't I just be happy*? she thought.

"Syd, chil' get up. You just gone sleep yo day away? Uh, uh honey, it is time to rise and shine. Boo open them curtains let the sunshine in here or at least the little that's left of it. Get up honey," Alex said moving closer to the bed.

"Babe calm down, let her get her barring's about herself. Would you go get her a drink of water?" Shawn asked Alex as he walked over to the bed closer to Syd.

"Good plan. Her hair already fucked up. If she don't get up, I'll just dash her with it. Good thinking," he said as he sashayed out of the bedroom.

"Syd, honey, are you okay? You were crying in your sleep. What's going on? Do you want to talk about it?" Shawn asked as he helped her sit up in bed.

"No, I'm fine, just a terrible dream I was having. I'm glad I woke up, thanks. What time is it, have you guys seen my cell?" Syd asked as she sat up, looking around the room, re-acclimating herself to today's reality and not the things in La La Land.

"Its 3:42. We have to be at the restaurant by 5:00 and by the looks of your hair, you will be thanking us for waking you," Shawn said patting the sides of her air dried naturally curly hair.

"Damn, I was sho looking forward to dashing yo ass with this water. Okay what's the T girl? Get up honey," "Alex said in a lively, vibrant tone. So what are we wearing? Are we going with a short showy dress, a long sophisticated dress, a business professional pants suit, an everyday dress? Honey stop me when I hit it."

"Oh my, that's a lot to take in when you just wake up. Can I find something to throw on, seeing as though I am nude under here?" Chryssany asked making eye contact with Alex.

"Chile I have seen every nook and cranny on that body, so of course I am only not leaving, but it's up to you and Shawn what he does," Alex said waving Shawn off.

"Well, I'm sure there is something I can find in the front to do," Shawn said standing and walking out of her bedroom.

"Thanks Shawnny bunny," she said winking at him. "Okay, so I'm going to the bathroom to do what I need to do in there, like brush my teeth, pull this hair into a bun and put my face on."

"Good, I'm going in the closet to find what I think you should wear. How you feeling like, a cute sun dress something fitted, hello? I feel like I just said all of this?" Alex said walking into her closet, looking around for something that might suit his likes.

"I'm feeling sexy, so something that accentuates my figure," she yelled as she pulled her hair up.

"Okay," he said taking out a red and black oriental style straight dress with some ten inch black red bottoms. "Okay, so how about this?" he said walking into the bathroom.

"Okay," she said taking the dress sliding it past her fresh up do.

Helping her pull the dress down, he took a step back, "Um, Chryssany what is this bulge you have going on in the front?" he said with a curious look on his face.

"What are you talking about?" she said walking over to her full-length mirror. "What is that? Oh, my! I guess its diet time," she said walking away from the mirror. "Something a little less tight," she giggled.

"Honey, you need maternity wear. Maternity wear aisle one!" he yelled to get Shawn's attention.

"Stop it, Alex! You play too much, "she said still looking in the mirror. *I really need to get this checked out. When was my last cycle?* she thought. *What if I am? Oh my, whose is it? But, I can't be. Maybe this is bloating and my cycle is on the way.*

"Are you okay"? Shawn said interrupting her thoughts as he walked back in.

"Huh? Oh, nothing," she said still in a daze.

"Your lips were moving, and no words were coming out. Is this about your dream?" He moved closer to her. "Talk to me, sweetie. I am here or would you like to wait until…"

"Later, yes," she said as she looked over his shoulder noticing Alex on his way back into the bathroom.

"Okay, honey, this dress still will kill those shoes, and it won't show whatever you have going on over there," he said summing up her situation up with a simple clasp of his hand.

"This is lovely, Syd it suits you well," Shawn said holding the dress close to her body.

"Okay, thanks. I will be out in a shake of a lamb's tail," she said pushing them both out of her restroom. She slid her dress off and over her head. Then on with a short, black sweetheart cut dress, with red roses embellished in a pin striped pattern. She walked over to her full-length mirror holding her breathe, not wanting to see her belly protruding. Her mind began to race once more about what if there is a baby in there? *Who's the father? Colby, he did have unprotected sex or at least I think, Damion, we never use protection, maybe my late night visitor. Oh my, what was I thinking*? Her stomach began to get queasy. *And I can't deal with this,* she thought. *How could I be so stupid*? She ran to the toilet as the vomit started coming up and out.

"Syd, are you okay? What happened?" Alex said grabbing a towel out of her linen closet?

"I don't know. My nerves are getting the best of me right now. Ugh I hate this crap."

"Are you sure there's no baby in there? Chile, you got more than enough symptoms," Alex said.

Syd attempted to give him the side-eye, but the vomit just kept coming.

"What do you need? Can I get you something? How long have you been like this?" Shawn questioned

"I don't know, I guess it was all of a sudden I don't know, just please make it stop."

Alex had disappeared and come back. "Here honey, drink this. I never knew why you kept ginger ale, but I am sure glad you have it."

Syd took a last heave, got up, walked over to her sink rinsed her mouth, took the ginger ale, and guzzled it down. "Thank you," she said out of breath, followed by a huge belch. "Oh, that feels better. Almost better than an Alka-Seltzer. What time is it?"

"Oh, it's 4:49," Shawn said casually.

"We have to go," Chryssany said in a panic.

"Yeah, we do babe," Alex said rushing out of the bathroom.

"Are you okay, boo?" Shawn asked before they walked out the bathroom.

"Yeah, I'm good," she replied with a smile.

"Babe, get in the car," Alex said yelling from the kitchen.

"Oh, I'm driving myself. I have a little appointment tonight after" she said with a wink.

"That's why yo ass, throwing up?" Alex said rolling his eyes.

"Ugh, whatever," she said paying him no attention.

"Yo ass know you ain't got nothing to do tonight. You just want a quick escape if shit get real," Alex said as Shawn went out the door.

"Either way, I'm driving myself. How about those apples?" she responded picking up her keys waving them behind her. "Lock the door behind you."

Syd got in her car, backed out of her garage, let it down, and balled as Shawn followed, who was driving like he was on a police chase, to the restaurant. He passed a parking spot at the door for her as he let Alex out. As she gathered her purse, she called Mel, and got out of her truck. "Okay, so we're here on time. Where the heck are you?" Syd questioned as she walked in looking around the restaurant.

"We're in the back, in the private area. It's already set up. Why you getting all up in arms? Just calm down," Mel said trying to get her to shut up.

"Well, where the menus at because I need a drink, honey, especially if this night will be anything like the one we had when we all met up the last time."

"Oh, your drama king? He's trying to make amends, so just accept the apology and move on," Syd said walking towards the private area.

"Honey, don't snip me up," Alex said as he sashayed behind her through the restaurant.

"Y'all sit over here, due to the situation, I mean ya know," Mel said seating Shawn and Alex close to the exit while side-eyeing Alex.

"You an ol' petty bitch," Alex said snatching his chair out. "I don't know why the fuck he put this bitch in charge of anything. Her people skills are slim to none, DAMN," he huffed as he folded his arms and crossed his legs as his foot began to shake.

"Fuck you, Alex," Mel said as she flipped him off walking across the room to make sure there was ample room between everyone, not wanting a repeat of what happened at the so-called breakfast.

"You never had a chance, bitch," Alex hissed as he rolled his eyes.

"Hell, she didn't either," Mel laughed as she pointed at Syd.

"Why even involve me in the foolishness?" Syd asked as she recounted the place settings. "Are we sure Shamika is coming?" she said in a more than stressed breath.

"Yeah, she is. And where she sitting at?" Shamika said as she waddled through the door.

"Oh, y'all seats over there by the restroom. I know she got her needs," Mel faked smiled as she pointed to the seats by the restroom.

"Um, where the service at? I need a damn drink, shit," Alex said waving his hand looking around.

"I know, right? I need a drink to deal with all these fake ass people. Damn, I wish I could," Shamika said rubbing her stomach.

"Mika that was so uncalled for," Damion said looking at her shocked and amazed by how ghetto she really was.

"It's fine, at least we know how she feels," Shawn said staring a hole into Shamika's soul.

"Okay, so yeah, restroom? I need to go, excuse me," Syd said as she walked passed Damion.

"Yeah, me too," Shamika said with her eyebrow raised.

Damion, grabbed her elbow, "Try anything, and I swear..." he said through gritted teeth.

Shamika snatched away laughing, "What bay?" she said walking away.

"See, I'm gone choke this hoe," Mel said watching them walk into the bathroom. As the door closed, she asked Damion," How much do you think you love this bitch because tonight is the night," she winked as she stood and walked in the bathroom.

"You think after this baby comes he still will want you? You think he's going to come for you? No, simple ass, because I have his blood, his son; back the fuck off," Shamika said cornering Syd in the handicap stall.

"No, Miss Ghetto Universe, you back off. You have to first be sure that is his baby. Then you have to be sure your months add up. See college isn't the only place I studied. I still study law, and I occasionally get paternity cases and more often than not, the chic lies about how many months she is because she's 'showing,'" Syd said walking out of the corner. "So recount those months, honey, and recount that man and the times. I, unlike you, am perfectly intelligent and am not blinded by whatever it is he sees in you," Syd pushed her out of the stall. "So, yea, I have to pee, and unless you plan on assisting me wiping this vagina, back off," Syd closed the door.

Mel began to cackle loud and uncontrollably as she walked out of the restroom. "I don’t know who that was in there, but I like her," she said as she wiped her eyes and walked back to her seat. "So where them drinks at?”

"Dish, bitch," Alex said putting his hands together as if to compose his excitement.

"Miss Girl, grew a pair," Mel said waving toward the restroom. "I guess you knocked some sense into her Tino," she said attempting to high-five him.

"Mel, don’t," Tino said putting his head in his hands. "This is supposed to be my apology dinner. You’re going to make it worse. Damn, Mel, just watch your fucking mouth," he said looking up.

"Damn, I thought everybody knew by now. I didn’t know we kept secrets," Mel said rolling her eyes. "Um, excuse me, Sir, SIR, yeah, you," she said as motioned for the waiter.

"Yes ma’am, my name is Colin. How may I help you?" the waiter asked.

"Yes, honey, I need a stiff drank," Alex said as the waiter walked swiftly passed him.

Shawn walked over to the ladies' room, "Syd, lady are you okay? You’ve been in here a while."

"Yeah, just not feeling too well honey, thank you," she responded through held back breathes.

"Damn, I'm okay, too," Shamika said as she pushed passed him.

"Great," he said as he dropped the door on her. "I'm coming in Boo, okay?"

"Yeah, okay," Syd responded.

He walked into the handicapped stall, "Hey what's going on?"

"I don't know. I am trying so hard to be the person I'm used to being, but this other person keeps slipping out. I refuse to apologize because in my mind it's what I wanted to say, but felt it was inappropriate to; but it came out anyway," she shrugged.

"It's called being fed up, honey. Don't feel bad. Her ass deserved whatever you gave her and some. Hone, shake it off. You are only the cutest chic here. So," he said holding his hand out, "What do you say? Wait you did wash that?" he said quickly snatching his hand away.

"Yes silly, I just came back in here. I don't want to be angry, mean, and/or bitter I want to be my happy vibrant self," she said walking out of the stall.

"You can be ALL that," he said summing it up in an unassuming slip of the wrist. "You can stand up for yourself and be vibrant. It just shows you don't take no mess, boo. It’s all good," he said winking walking out of the restroom.

"We already ordered y’all food and drink, "she said with a little too much attitude.” So Syd, when were we going to find out Valentino knocked yo ass out?" Alex asked standing rolling his neck and folding his arms.

"Wait, what?" Shawn asked in with a confused look on his face.

"Look, first and foremost you don’t know nor do you understand the parameters surrounding the incident so don’t question me about it. Next, Mel keep your mouth shut, gosh. You all need to understand we are here for a meaningful and loving reason, not to bicker and fight. Damn, you all can’t get it right to save each other, huh? I accept whatever apology you may have for me babe, I love you, but I have things to do tomorrow and need to plan. All of you need to be ashamed; he’s freaking family," Syd said snatching her purse storming out.

"Well, okay, she’s right," Damion finally spoke up. "Lil Bruh, it is what it is. Love you homie," he said to Valentino as they shook hands into an embrace.

"Thanks, man," he said to Damion. "To y’all, I know what I could have caused and I apologize for all the things that happened and all the words exchanged," he said hoping they saw it was heartfelt. "I realized it was a total mistake."

"A'ight enough of that. Are we all straight?" Mel said looking around to get a nod from everyone. "Good," she said as she gave them the thumbs up. "I will talk to Miss Thing tomorrow. I don't know what she got going on."

"Here's all the food," Colin, the waiter entered with a couple others. "Salmon, corn, broccoli?"

"To go," Alex and Shawn said in unison.

The waiter turned to respond to Alex and Shawn as he titled a strawberry lemonade onto Mel's shoe.

Startled Mel kicked the waiter, "Oh, my. I'm so... my apologies, sir. Wow that was cold."

"Oh, so the jail bird got manners?" Shamika said laughing harder than she should.

"Bitch, here you some manners," Mel got up reached across the table and slapped the shit out of Shamika. "How you like them apples, bitch?" Mel said gathering mucousy saliva from her throat.

"Oh, see bitch you..." Shamika jumped up reached across the table and grabbed Mel by her collar. Mel spit directly into Shamika's face. "Um, gone kill this bitch," Shamika screamed attempting to wrap her hand in Mel's hair. Mel reached back with her fist balled and tried to knock the daylights out of Shamika. Valentino whisked around the table, grabbing Mel.

"Mel please, think. This bitch ain't worth it. Please think," Valentino pleaded, looking her in the eyes." I hurt you just as much as I have them, and this is not the way. Let's come to a resolve, me and you not her. Fuck her. Please," he said as if he and she were the only two in the room.

"I am going to get that bitch," Shamika said trying to get around the table. "Bitch, I hope they still have your cell open because you're going back."

"Shut up, chil'. Do you not value your life or your child's well-being? Obviously, she don't so have a seat or leave. Please rethink your strategy Shamika," Alex said explaining Shamika's current situation to her.

"Babe, calm down. Think about our child. Let's go, I will take care of you," Damion said trying to calm Shamika down. "Just wait until we get home, babe. It will be you and me. Whatever you want. I will do whatever you want, just please calm down. You're putting the baby at risk," he said gently placing his hand on her baby bump.

"You're right," she said putting down the napkin she wiped her face with. "These lonely ass hoes going home alone and I have it all. I'm ready to leave now Damion," Shamika demanded.

"Please, take this side piece, replacement gone wrong home, before I beat that bitch," Mel said cracking her knuckles.

"Mel," Damion growled.

"What?" she replied simply. "I ain't forgot, and bitch you on my list. So you might want to back down," she said squaring up with him.

"Let me get the check," he said grabbing his jacket and attempting to get his wallet.

"No, let these miserable bitches pay for it. Let's go now!" she said grabbing his arm, walking towards the exit. "Why would you let her say that," Shamika asked as they walked out?

Doctor's Office

"Mel, I don't know what's wrong with me, but my stomach has been in knots for a few weeks now, around the time Alex and Shawn came back in town. I know it isn't them, but man this isn't right. Maybe it was something I ate."

"Girl that was more than a month and a half ago. Whatever you ate has passed through your system. You sure it's not one of the cases you working on or a house? Are all your bills paid up? Or will you be the last to find out that you pregnant," she asked concerned and a bit taken aback by what might be.

"Come on, Mel you know me better than that; you know all my shit together. These cases don't get to me anymore. I do my very best to hold up justice, but it is what it is. And all my houses are practically selling themselves, or that's what my agents say. So I am straight ma'am," Syd said reassuring her. "If I were pregnant, I am sure I would know, so you guys can keep all the non-sense to yourselves," she said dismissing the idea, or even the thought, of being pregnant.

"Well, what are the symptoms? Hell, you might JUST be pregnant," Mel said sarcastically in an effort to strike a nerve with Syd.

"That's not in the least funny; you know what happened with Cordney, and after all the accusations, dang," she said seriously. "But I get nauseated all the time and vomit a lot. Hell, I might have a stomach virus. I don't want to go to the doctor. They might say something I don't want to hear."

"But, if it is a virus you better go get checked out before it's too late. You might be dying. Hell, you didn't stay at the hospital so they could check you out," she said seriously with a perplexed look on her face. "Come to think of it, did they ever call you back? You never let me know anything about that," Mel said reminiscing about the days passed.

Syd replied, trying to suppress a laugh, "Girl, whatever. If I were dying, Mel, I wouldn't be going out with you tonight. You know, I am just fine."

"Well, to be on the safe side, I'll call Dr. Hardy because she'll know," she said taking out her phone. "Hey, Gwen, Can I make an appointment for Chryssany? This is Melony."

"Yes ma'am, Ms. Melony," Gwen said politely.

"Today, if possible, please," Mel said hurriedly.

"Oh, okay. Let Ms. Jackson know her appointment is for 2:00 o'clock."

"Damn, oh, excuse me, but its 1: 30 now," Mel said.

"Yes ma'am, that's the soonest appointment we have. Is that too soon?" Gwen asked.

"No, no we'll be there in a moment. Thanks," Mel said hanging up the phone.

"Girl, come on. We ain't got time to talk. Come on. Thirty minutes to get you signed in and all that good stuff," Mel said with a bit of urgency in her voice.

"Already? Okay, let me change," Syd said walking towards her bedroom

"Honey, you don't have that kind of time," she said grabbing her arm pulling her towards the door.

"Alright Mel," she said defensively, getting into her truck

"My bad Syd, but come on, you can't get sick. I need you to be okay," Mel said almost crying.

"Girl, I didn't know you cared like that," Syd said surprised.

"You know I am trying to get married, and you are the only reason besides him of course. But, girl you have to be okay. You are my best friend!"

"Okay, Mel. I am the sensitive one so stop now. When you panic, I panic, and we can't do this girl. You know this is it turn…. TURN."

"Don't panic. Chill, I don't turn into that drive cause of that big ass hole. Here's the one I turn into. What has you on pins and needles?" Mel asked like she didn't know.

"Look, Mel, you know what happened with Cordney, and I pray I'm not pregnant because I'm going to have to abort it. I'm not ready for children. I'm not even married," Syd said with a big sigh.

"You sure he's the only candidate for yo baby's daddy?" she asked real suspicious like.

"What the hell you mean, Mel? I ain't no ho. Hell, I don't remember sleeping with Cordney. I remember the night, but I don't remember anything he said; as a matter of fact I ended up at yo house that night because he was trying to spend da night," Syd said justifying about to cuss her ass out.

"Well, look Syd, I'm not supposed to say anything, but hell you need to know. I talk to Damion everyday about you, not to be a matchmaker or anything…."

"Oh, I know he got his match," Syd said interrupting her.

"Shut up and listen, Syd! He loves you, and he told me when he spent the night, you and him sexed all night and all day without protection. No, you don't have anything," Mel said responding to the look of shock on her friend's face, "but he was trying to get you pregnant."

Syd unbuckled her seatbelt looked, at Mel with tears her my eyes, opened the door, stepped out, and looked back at her and said, “Friend, I’ll get a ride home,” closed the door and walked into the office doors and as she glanced back, Mel had picked up the phone. "Who the hell could she be calling?"

Syd signed in and took a seat. She sat down with a million thoughts running through her mind. *How dare she do this to me? What was she thinking, and what was he thinking? These are supposed to be my best friends. I don’t believe this shit. Damn!*

"Ms. Jackson?" Nicole the nurse bellowed.

"Yes," she said standing with spaghetti legs.

"Can you fill this cup to the line and place it in the window seal?" asked Nicole.

"Yes, ma’am," Syd answered as she had done many times before, thinking nothing of this part of the visit. She did as instructed and walked into the examination room.

"Please undress, and put on this gown for your examination," Nicole asked.

Carefully folding her under garments into her clothes so they weren't visible and/or wouldn't fall out at an inappropriate time, she thought of the moments with Damion, the way he felt, his cologne, how she loved every moment of him. He had been her standard for the guys she had dated all her life. *How could he do this to me?* Tears filled her eyes. Shaking her head and rocking, she thought, *I don't believe this*. She started reading a couple of articles, trying to change her thoughts of what may be about to happen. *My life can't change like this. I don't know what to do. It's nothing just a little bug*, her mind raced. *What if I am pregnant and it isn't Damion' and it's Cordney's? What would I do, God knows I don't believe in abortion?* She began to pray:

God, please help me understand what's happening. I know you set this up for my good, but God, please send me a sign. I don't know how to accept this! Please just let this be stress. Oh, God I don't know....

Dr. Hardy entered the exam room, startling her right out of prayer mode. "Good afternoon, Ms. Jackson. Your urine analysis came back positive, but I would like to get a blood test as well as an ultrasound for reassurance. "

"Okay, let's get the correct results please and thank you," she said anxious to get a negative.

She began by drawing blood; Nicole came in and collected the sample. "Lay back for me, Ms. Jackson," Dr. Hardy Instructed. "This gel is a bit chilly, ready?"

Syd shook my head yes.

"Okay, you hear that? That's your child's heartbeat. Congratulations, Ms. Jackson. You're about nine weeks pregnant," Dr. Hardy said.

Tears formed in her eyes and she began to hyperventilate. "What?" she said, trying to regain her regular breathing pattern.

"Yes, ma'am, you right at two months pregnant. Would you like for me to go over your options?" she asked with concern.

"No, ma'am, I know them. Thank you for confirming," she said gathering her things. The doctor left the room. Syd slowly dressed herself thinking, *this has to be an out of body experience or a dream. Oh, God somebody wake me up.*

She walked out of the doors into the waiting room and Melony was standing there with open arms. Mel looked at her and instantly knew what was said. She grabbed Syd as she fell into her arms. She wrapped her arms around and whispered in her ear, "Whatever you want to do I support you, friend." "Well support keeping this between me and you," Syd said, wiping her eyes.

"Not even yo baby daddy," she said sarcastically. Syd gave her a menacing look and she instantly stopped smiling. "Well what are we going to do?" she asked with a concerned look on her face.

"I got this," Syd said with a no worries tone as they headed towards the door.

She looked at her friend and said, "Okay, as long as you got it together."

"I do," Syd said faking confidence, then thought to herself, *Now what am I gonna do?* as she was walking out the door.

"So, if you don't mind me asking, who is the baby daddy? I know you know. I saw you're 'my days' calendar. Initials and hearts don't mean you bleeding. I know of a couple possibilities. Cordney," she said gauging Syd's reaction, slowly continuing, "Damion," she said in an upbeat tone, again gauging Syd's reaction. "Baby girl, is there anyone else?" she asked sympathetically.

Syd just sat back and cried. Through the tears, she asked, "How could I let this happen? Why me? I can't believe I could be so stupid. What will my dad say? My mother? Oh, God," the tears kept flowing. "What am I going to do?" she said, falling apart.

"You are going to let it out, clear your mind, relax, relate, and release," Mel said driving carefully watching the road and eyeing Syd from time to time. "Do you want food?" she asked eyeing the restaurants.

"No," Syd said putting her face in her hands, trying to rub the stress away from her face. "Just take me home. I have to take care of some things, to sort some stuff out."

"K, boo. Are you sure, though?" she asked genuinely concerned.

"Yeah, I just need to think through this now," she said trying to come up with a master plan.

"Okay, well don't go committing suicide. I need my friend and new little person, okay?" she said almost seriously.

"Chile, I am a little sad, shocked, and very surprised, but suicidal? Honey, you have no worries of that. I am still at one-hundred percent on life though," Syd said with a little giggle.

"Well, as long as you are laughing. I would hate to take that detour to lakeside," she said getting off on my exit.

"Lakeside? You know me better than that!" she said rethinking the friendship.

"Well, here you are, home," she said racing into the estates Syd lived in.

"Oh, well thanks, 'friend'" she said side-eyeing her. "I will call if I need you."

Syd jumped out and raced in the house. Syd waved her off as Mel sped away.

Syd grabbed her phone as soon as she got in, "Mel! Mel! MEL! I went from zero to a hundred."

"What?" she yelled back. "What's going on?" she asked in an anxious tone.

"This is my freaking business, so please don't share it, I greatly appreciate it!!!!" Syd said in the most serious voice she could muster.

"Okay", she said, "Damn, why would you.... Well, aight. I got you. No one will know. Your secret is safe with me this time, I promise."

"Thanks," Syd said starting her car.

"Where you going? What you doing, Chryssany? Hello? Hello?" Syd heard her say as she hung up.

She sat in her garage for a minute thinking about exactly what she was going to say, where she was going, then she put my car in drive, and let Musiq take control. The sultry sounds guided her safely through those Memphis streets and right to Damion's front door. So she got out and rang the bell. The door opened …

"He ain't here, but come in. I been wanting to talk to you anyway," Shamika said.

"With the day I have been having, ugh, whatever. What's up?" Syd said as she entered her friend's home.

"What's up is you and MY man. I know it has to hurt that he chose me over you, but get over it. You can't compete with a baby. You don't weigh up," she said. "Oh, and stop popping up and calling him. It's pathetic, you know, for you to be this 'big time lawyer.' You have a shitty way of taking care of your own business."

Syd squared up with her. "You nothing having, baby momma, manipulating, bottom feeding, welfare receiving, broken English speaking ass bitch need to learn to stay in your lane. See, its simple hoes like you that show me what could have been me."

"Oh, you mean living the lavish life?" she interrupted.

"No, bitch one meal away from a shelter, one wrong word away from the poor house, one fuck up away from being fucked up. So please don't tell me how to live my life, where to go, or who to call because you simply don't weigh up. Silly ass. You better hope that's his baby. Word around town is it's not definite, but again we will see what's in store for you and that baby," Syd said walking away. "And you might want to watch what you say; I still got pull with YO man. Fuck up simple ass bitch, matter of fact get the classifieds. You may need to start saving because I hear the shit that happens in shelters to little kids can be brutal," Syd slammed the front door. As she walked to her car, she saw Damion pulling up, but simply got into her truck and drove away. "Fuck them." She turned on her K. Michelle "No Fucks Given" catering to her ratchet side.

Damion walked into the house. "Who was that?" he asked Shamika.

She sucked her teeth, "Yo bitch."

"Was it Mel or Syd?" he asked ignoring her attitude.

"Pick one and shut the fuck up talking to me," she said walking up the steps. "Nawl," she said turning around. "You need to tell that bitch, Chryssany, this is my fucking house, I ain't going no damn where. I almost slapped the bitch. She better be lucky I'm pregnant," she said rubbing her stomach.

"That was Chryssany? What happened, Shamika?" he said with his jaw clinched.

"I just told her; you, mine and she need to back off," she said looking away.

"You did what?" he said, grabbing his keys walking back out the door. "I ain't coming back tonight."

"It's already late. Where you going? You know what? Run to the bitch you better pray I'm here when you get back," she said threatening him.

"You better pray I want you here when I get back," he said one-upping her, getting into his car.

"Damn, damn, damn, ugh," he picked up his phone and dialed Chryssany's number. No answer. He called back what seemed like a hundred times. He pulled in her driveway. No car. No Syd. "Where is she? Shit. Where could she be," he thought aloud. Pulling out of her driveway, he picked up his phone again and dialed Mel. "Mel answer, please answer."

"Hello, what's up?" Mel answered.

"Have you talked to Chryssany lately?" he asked in an exasperated tone.

"Not since earlier. Why what happened? I knew I shouldn't leave her alone," she said panicking.

"No, she came by today and her and Shamika had words. I don't know exactly what was said but, damn it was serious, at least Mika seemed to think so."

"Oh, this is about her. I don't mean no harm, but fuck that lame ass bitch," she said yawning in the phone.

"NO, it's about..." he started.

"Goodnight." She hung up.

He kept driving and thinking, "Damn, what happened? Chryssany is my dream, but Shamika has my seed. How can I be a man and not do what's right?"

He pulled into Mel's subdivision, hopped out of the car, briskly walked to the door, and rang the bell about three times.

"What it is?" Mel said with one hand behind her back concealing a small twenty-two.

"I love her. I love the way she smells, the way she talks, the way when she's mad her voice gets squeaky, I love making love to her. I need her, Mel," Damion said continuing his thoughts.

"Um, look dude, it's kinda nippy outside," Mel said clutching her robe and opening the door so Damion could come in, "and I would love to talk to you, but you gone have to come inside. Now exactly who is it you talking about?" Mel asked concerned.

"I want to tell her about the proposal and the pregnancy. You know, Shamika said she was pregnant. So I have to be a man and take care of mine," Damion said sadly.

"Negro, you just confused the hell outta me. What the fuck is you saying?" Mel said irritated, walking into the kitchen to make some tea.

Damion followed her into the kitchen, sat on a bar stool, and continued to spill his guts. "I was talking about Syd at first, then her. I don't know what to do. Should I tell Chryssany or just let shit happen? I mean I haven't proposed to Mika yet, but I plan to, especially if she carrying my baby. But what about my soul mate, my one true love?" Damion asked talking in circles again.

Mel poured them both a glass of tea and asked, "You sure it's yours? You said y'all been using protection right?"

Damion shook his head while saying, "Look, I was always careful, but the condom broke more than a few times. A nigga start getting lazy and going to the corner store. No Magnum, next best thing."

"Well that's yo dumb ass, but if some shit go down with Chryssany I'm gone kick yo ass and Mika ass. You got her fucked up. Listen to yourself; you love her, but she's pregnant. I'm not mad I just don't understand what you expect me to say." Mel put her cup down and began weighing his options as if they were in her hands. "If I were Mika's ass I'd be hurt, but knowing Syd she'd understand. Her feelings might be hurt at first, but she'll understand. So I guess what I'm trying to say is, congratulations you gone be somebody daddy and husband. I'm so proud of you. Look at you all grown up."

"Damn, thanks Mel cause I was fucked up," Damion said getting up like a huge weight had been lifted off his shoulders. "You know I don't drink no damn tea. Stop playing," he said laughing, walking towards the door.

"So you want me to tell Chryssany or you gone tell her?" Mel asked.

Damion froze in his tracks, "DON'T SAY SHIT. I'm gone tell her the next time I see her."

"Yeah whatever, but I got you," Mel said closing the door and sucking her teeth. "All these damn secrets."

Damion got into his car. With his mind racing, he put in a mixed cd with three playas on it; R. Kelly, Lloyd, and Trey Songz. He headed home. In letting the music soothe his soul and clear his mind, all the while weighing his options himself, He began to think of life with Shamika, beautiful light skinned chic half Puerto Rican half black, but 100% trifling. He loved her because of where she came from and she triumphed where a lot of other people would have fallen or given up. Shamika's mom was Puerto Rican and her dad was ashy black. Her dad was a small time gangsta who made her mom turn tricks to feed him. When Shamika became of age, her dad tried to do the same shit to her but she wasn't having it. Shamika had been on her own for a very long time doing what was necessary to make ends meet. That's until she met Damion. She thought he was just some lowly trick that she'd get some money from and keep it moving. But instead, he treated her like a real person, not just some ass. He didn't expect sex after dinner. He wanted to get to know her first. She let her guard down and got comfortable living the good life, but when they fought and her lively hood was at stake, she reverted back to her old ways of the streets. That's why he couldn't be to sure if the baby was his or not.

On the other hand, he has Chryssany, a no nonsense type bitch; she was born and raised in the hood, too. She never got caught up in any shit because the hood had love for her. She was his first hell; they took each other's virginity after graduation senior year. She had been there for him since ninth grade, was even there when his grandmother passed, and held him every night until he fell asleep. She stood on her own. He didn't ever have to worry about her having her hand out or embarrassing him in front of his professional peers. She was a professional and a gangsta. She knew the right time for it all. And that's why he loved her.

Damion walked into the house to find Mika's trifling ass hadn't cleaned up shit and had the nerve to wanna fire the maid. "Shamika!" he yelled through the house. "Where you at?"

"I'm up here, Daddy," she said in the saddest baby voice possible.

He walked up the steps picking up her clothes and shoes all the way up. "Why the hell ain't you done cleaned up?" he asked putting the clothes in the hamper.

"Baby, you know I am pregnant and can't do all that stuff no more," she said whining.

"You ain't that damned pregnant, Mika. Get up off yo lazy ass and clean this shit up," he said irritated.

"Who the hell you yelling at nigga? I will cut yo ass," she said with a heavy Puerto Rican accent.

"Do what you gotta baby, but you better have somewhere to go after that cause ya ass can't stay here," he yelled back at her.

"Damn, that was cold hearted Damion, and it's kinda fucked up you would say something like that to the woman that's having your child" she said manipulatively.

"Baby, you know I didn't mean it like that. I love you Mika, but this house needs to stay clean. What if you trip going down the steps because you left some clothes or shoes and lost the baby? What if that happened or something worse? That's all I'm saying," he said apologetically.

"Will you help me, Daddy?" she asked in a baby voice.

"You know it. I'll start downstairs," he said looking her in the eyes.

She smiled real big and headed into the bathroom to clean herself up; she came back out and called out to him, "Baby where are you?"

"I'm downstairs," he said with a light chuckle.

"You make me sick," she whined.

He finished cleaning the main rooms downstairs and headed up to help her to only find her fast asleep. He finished cleaning, showered, and crawled into bed. He wrapped his arms around her, and put his member in the crack of her ass, trying to wake her for some late night cuddy.

"No, stop it," she said as she shifted away from him and out of his arms.

He simply rolled over and daydreamed of his last moments with Chryssany and how she never said no.

He awakened to his cell phone ringing "Wonder Woman" ringtone. *That's Syd*, he thought. *I'm gone kill Mel's ass.* He picked it up trying to sound nonchalant and awake. "Hello?"

"Hey, boo. I likes that ring back 'Shawty I'm the Shit,'" she said singing off key. "I'm in your area and wanted to know if you were at home. Are you?" she asked.

"Yeah, what time is it?" he said rolling over, looking for Shamika.

"Oh, about noon. Are you still in bed," she asked? "Yep, but I'm getting up. I'm glad you called. I needed to talk to you anyway," he said hurriedly.

"Ooh, hold on, someone is on the other end," she said excitedly.

"Who is more important than me Chryssany Michelle? I am not going to hold on. Who is it?" he said impatiently.

"Look, I'm am about to stop and get something to eat. You want something? Backyard burger?" she said ignoring his ass

"Yep, same thang you getting," he said."

"Aight, fat ass," she said rushing off the phone, but it was too late because the other line had hung up. "Dang."

Damion got up to found Shamika fully dressed and she hadn't attempted to cook or straighten a damn thing. "Babe, where you going?" he asked her.

"My belly is getting bigger. You don't want me to wear my clothes little, do you?" she asked looking up at him. "And I want to start buying stuff for the nursery. Oh, and I got nauseated trying to finish cleaning, so I stopped. Where's the card?" she said bluntly

He looked at her and veins popped out of his neck. Through gritted teeth he said, "On the counter by the wash room."

"Thanks, baby." She kissed him on the cheek, went downstairs, grabbed the card and her keys.

Damion heard the garage door go up and said, "DAMN."

About ten minutes later his cellular phone rang. Again it was "Wonder Woman." "Whaddup?" he said sounding dreary.

"Oh, nothing just need you to open the door before I waste our stuff."

"Damn, I forgot you said you were in your way; I'm on my way down," he said.

"Hurry up, I don't want the rogues, thieves, and murderers to get me," she said with a laugh.

He ran down the steps and skipped the last three; he came to the door all sweaty like and grabbed everything she had out of her hands. "Come in Syd," he said leading her into his beautiful kitchen. He grabbed two plates and put the food on them and handed her a plate.

"Where is your better half?" she asked, looking around. "I don't want to be rude by not speaking."

"She just left, and what happened yesterday? I mean I am sorry about it," he said.

"Oh, no apology necessary. I said my piece and was done," she said as she took a big bite out of her burger.

"Damn, girl, slow down. It'll be there," he said jokingly. "We straight, though, right?"

"Of course, I don't blame you for her," she said taking a sip of her ginger ale.

"Okay, enough," Damion said. "Have you talked to Mel today?"

"Um, yeah, she's only my best friend. Why wouldn't I talk to her?" she ask sarcastically.

"Damn, a nigga was just asking," he said laughing. "Okay, what if I said something that went against everything I said to you that night we spent together before Alex came back?" he said clearing the table and standing by the bar.

"I wouldn't be surprised," she said.

"Well, look I am gonna apologize now again because I never meant to hurt you and I would never hurt you intentionally," he said.

"Okay, go ahead," she said impatiently.

"Okay, I am gonna ask Shamika to marry me because she is pregnant, and I am a man that takes care of his shit."

"Wow," she said in a high pitched voice. At that, she felt her heart drop and fall clean out her ass. Her eyes were wide and began to fill with tears. "Well, Damion, congratulations." She got up and walked towards his glass front door. The tears began to fall. He was walking her way.

"Chryssany, if you mad say so. If you hurt say so, curse or something. Don't just leave me like this," he pleaded.

She opened the door and said, "See you later friend," and closed it behind her.

"SHIT, what am I gone do? I can't hurt her like this she wouldn't hurt me like this," Damion said while picking up the phone to call Melony.

"Hello, Damion," she said plainly into the phone.

"I told her, and she just said 'Wow, and congratulations,' and walked out. Then said she'd talk to me later and called me friend. I saw her reflection in my door. She was crying, and I know she was upset because of how high her voice got. What am I gone do, Mel?" he pleaded.

"You are gonna suck it up. You know what's in your heart, so go for it," Mel said advising him.

"Damn, I didn't want to hurt her."

Syd's Week off

"There's a meeting this morning, Mr. Abernathy, and if you value your job, I suggest you be there," Syd said with a no nonsense tone walking through her Real Estate office.

"Yes, Ms. Jackson," he said with a smirk.

"Where is Toni?" she thought aloud walking into her office.

"I'm here, Ms. Jackson," she said standing from the couch and walking towards Syd's desk.

"Oh, great. How was your weekend?" she asked in a hurried tone.

"It was great. I took the twins to a waterpark. Skylar overcame his fears of the water while Dai as always enjoyed herself," she said with a faraway look and a pride Syd could only recognize because she had seen it on her mom's face a few times. "How was your weekend Ms. Jackson? Missed you in the office Friday."

"It was eventful," she said in a dismissive tone. "Did you get my emails pertaining to today's meeting?"

"I did. Everything is set up, just the way you asked," she said following Syd out of the office.

"Awesome, are all employees present, to your knowledge, that will benefit from this meeting? I ask this because last month there were a few discrepancies and unhappy employees. Good Morning," she spoke to the receptionist as she passed.

Syd entered the board room with her assistant Toni. "Please make sure all the water pitchers are full and there are ample breakfast snacks without wrappers because I would hate to be interrupted by that sound. I have given a specific list and would like your selections to correspond directly. I want my presentation to go exactly the way I delineated. I tried to be so precise, that at any point during my presentation, if needed, I could leave and you would have the ability to pick up. Is that a possibility for you Ms. Toni?" she asked in a stern demanding demeanor.

"Yes, is this because of your pregnancy?" Toni asked seemingly perplexed.

"Excuse me," Syd asked walking toward the door to close it.

"Well, I know that you are a workaholic and knowing that I have seen a few of your habits changed drastically. Your management style, while stern, is also very open. In stating that, Ms. Jackson, you have become a bit more reserved, not to mention that you frequent your personal lavatory much more often. Your eating habits have tremendously changed. Where you would eat a steak, you now replaced with much lighter food like a turkey sandwich, no soda, only water and ginger ale. Where most of the people here frown upon my having children before starting my career, I have the advantage. I have passed the hard part and can recognize the symptoms. I did not mean to offend you, I just noticed and for you to give me such an incredible task. There have to be some great extenuating circumstances."

Syd turned and began speaking in a low and unsympathetic tone. "Ms. Toni, although I appreciate your attention to detail in this moment, it is very much unsolicited and unwelcome. There is a professional line." She took a deep breath, noticing the tears forming. "Excuse me."

Toni came over and embraced her. "I may have overstepped, but ever since you hired me I have paid very close attention to you and your habits because I someday want to become a successful woman with a thriving business. I have learned so much from you. You don't really deal with emotion. You just simply close the door on it. This isn't something that you can just shut out."

"I know," she said, fighting back the tears. Taking a step back and gathering her emotions, she said, "Thank you, I really needed that. I would also greatly appreciate your clandestineness on the subject. Thank you in advance."

There was a tap on the door startling both of them. Syd continued to gather herself. "I'll get it," Toni said with a smile and nod, "and I'll take my time."

"Thank you," Syd mouthed while patting her face.

Clearing her throat, Toni said, "Ms. Jackson, there is a Mr. Thornton here to see you. Here you are, Mr. Thornton. Would you two like your office, as the conference room will soon be in use for our company wide meeting."

Taking a deep breathe, clearing her throat and mind, she smoothed her charcoal grey pencil skirt out while walking toward Mr. Thornton. "Thank you Toni, please lead my meeting as I would. I will be in my office if needed. Right this way," she motioned toward Greg. "It is surprising to see you after our last encounter. I assumed that we'd crossed paths for the last time," she said over her shoulder walking down the hall and into the office.

With a small chuckle, Greg said, "You can't get rid of me that easily. The different things we have endured through the years? This is just a hiccup." Closing the door behind him, he grabbed her arm, turned her around, and squeezed her in the most loving way she could have ever imagined.

"Wow," she said, freeing herself from the odd, but essential embrace. "Thank you, but really you know more than a lot of others. I thought my secret was safe. The last time I saw you, the look on your face said it all. What made you visit today?" she asked hurriedly.

"Because, you are all I can think of, and the load you're carrying, mentally and physically, can be more than one person can bear alone. I know you have your friends and how close you are with them, but I want to be your man," he said honestly.

"That's awesomely sweet, but are you sure you want to involve yourself in my mess? Like, I know there are many women who would love to be with a man like you," she said, hoping he would still want to be with and comfort her. "Why me?" she said walking toward the black and cream trimmed love seat in the corner of the office.

"Let me take you to lunch," he said walking towards her.

"When?" she asked surprised

"Now, tomorrow, the day after that, and forever if you want," he said sitting and wrapping his arms around her.

She couldn't stop the tears. "That is .... I don't know. Wow," she said at a loss for words.

"Just say yes, that's all I actually want to hear you say anyway," he said smiling with her still in his arms.

"Well, in that case yes, yes, and yes," she said returning his embrace. In an instant stopping, she said, "If we meet later down the line and my people are around, this has to replay. My happily ever after will be public," she smiled gazing into his eyes.

"Great," he said standing them both up. "If I ever get the chance to make you fall for me publicly, I promise you'll never forget it," he pressed his lips against hers softly enough to taste the gloss, but firmly enough for her tongue to part his lips and tease his. Gently releasing himself from the kiss, he thought he would never get again he said, "I'll get my car while you tie up your loose ends in the office."

She messaged Toni, "I will be out of the office until further notice," gathered her things, and high-tailed it to the elevator.

As she pressed the button to go down, she could only think, *God is trying to tell me something, and I would be foolish not to listen. I have not seen this man in a few years and yet here he is, the same wonderful, caring guy he was all that time ago*. "Let's see where this goes", she said as she exited the elevator to be surprised with a dozen mixed colored roses. "Wow, what did I do to deserve these?" she asked.

"You said yes, and I promise you will never regret it," he said opening his car door for her.

The Barbeque

The phone is ringing and I know she hears it. Why ain't she answering it? Damn girl PUHLEAZ answer the phone.

"Hello Chryssany, what's up? Have you started having them cravings yet? Pickles and ice cream and all that good stuff? I am so excited! I am finally gonna be an aunt. And where the hell you been? Real friends talk daily. It has been almost a week since we went to the doctor, and I have not heard from you. What's up with that? Is everything okay? You still…right? Hello??" Melony said answering the phone.

"Hey, girl. I miss and love you, too. There are a lot of things going on, and it feels like I have a million things on my plate, and now my clothes are starting to fit funny, and my moods have become increasingly aggravating these days. And yes, I would never do that. You know me better than that, ma'am and…

I think I am starting to show. I don't know what to do. I want to tell him, but he has a fiancée and family, and I think, I'm gonna tell people I went to a sperm bank and got artificial inseminated."

"Girl you so silly. Why can't you just tell him? I'll tell him to gauge his reaction, then say I was just trying to see what he would say," Mel said trying to lighten the mood.

"Don't do that. That is so juvenile, and I am pregnant, and I'm sure once he sees me, after the statement, the shit will hit the fan," Syd said in a "girl please" voice.

"Yeah, you right. Hold on. I am receiving another call," Mel said in a proper voice.

"Aight ma'am," Syd said ghetto fabulous like.

"Hello, this is Melony. Hey D.," Mel said happily.

"What's up, Ms. Melony? What you up to?" Damion asked.

"Nothing. On the other line with Chryssany. What's up with you, Mr. Almost Married?" she asked sweetly.

"Who almost married? I have not proposed to anyone, so I'm dating. How is Chryssany? I haven't heard from her in about a month. As a matter of fact, conference me in, I want to holla at her," Damion said waiting

"Okay, hold let me, hold on," Mel said a bit agitated, wondering if she should tell Syd that Damion is on the phone or not before Mel conferences the call and then made a quick decision not to.

"Okay... hello," Mel said.

"Hello," Damion and Syd said in unison.

"Hey, Syd. I haven't heard from you in a while. How are you?" Damion asked.

"I'm fine, a little on the sick side, but I'll live," she replied before adding, "I'm gonna kill you Mel", under her breath

"I ain't call him. He called me," Mel said defensively.

"What, you didn't to wanna talk to me or something?" Damion asked Syd.

"Nothing like that. We were just having a conversation and I needed her advice that's all," Syd said trying to clean up her death threat.

"Oh, well, I was calling to invite you to a cook out I'm having today, and don't start that I ain't coming mess because I am not having it," Damion said in a no-nonsense voice.

Mel quickly said, "We'll be there."

Syd said, "Well, I ain't got nothing to wear, so I can't make it. Sorry, friend."

"Whatever. I said I ain't having it, and I meant it. I will come drag ya ass kicking and screaming if I have to. So now what?" Damion questioned Syd

"Okay, lemme..." she began to think of what she could wear.

Sundress that hides my belly, she thought to myself. "Alright, Me, I'm riding with you, and I need to go get something to wear," she said

"No time. It's already 8:00 o'clock. Find something in your closet and haul ass!" Damion demanded.

"Ugh, we'll be there in about an hour or so," Mel said.

"I can deal with that," Damion said.

"You ain't got no choice," Mel and I said at the same time laughing.

She disconnected the line and asked, "So what are you gone wear for real?"

"I don't know, something that doesn't show my stomach; I am not ready for this," Syd said stressing out

"Girl, stop. I already knew about the cookout and had planned on going. I knew you would have said no so I didn't ask. I got my clothes out, and I am almost ready to go. I am on my over there now."

"Okay, honey, please hurry because I am stressing out," Syd said, trying to calm down.

Syd laid down to rest her nerves and drifted into a new universe that only contained Damion and herself. He loved her and would be the perfect father to their child. *He's my husband, we're in bliss. Watching him rub my big belly, talking and sing to our baby. Man, this is the life. He loves me.*

"Chryssany Michelle, get your round belly ass up!!" Melony let herself in and yelled in her bedroom doorway.

Groggily she replied, "I am up, but I honestly have nothing to wear and it is making me a bit emotional. I kind of want to cry right now," she said misty eyed sitting up in the middle of the bed.

"I saw this coming soooo, I bought these. After that doctors appointment I was so excited and couldn't wait to see your little baby bump. So a Pea in a Pod has been calling my name for you. Here are three different dresses you can wear. Dress one a gorgeous powder blue, plunging neck and back, with intricate black designs," Mel said in the sweetest most sincere voice she had ever heard.

"Sold," Syd said fighting back tears. "I'll wear this one. You are hands down the best friend a girl could ever have. Thank you for having my back even when I obviously can't have it myself. I love you." Getting off her bed she headed into the shoe closet. "I have the cutest black strappy sandals to go with the details in that dress. I hope my pedicure doesn't clash."

"You will be fine, honey. You know I love you like a sister and I got to look out for you because Damion doesn't know, so he can't do it. By the way, have you talked to Alex about this? I am very interested in his opinion on the matter," she said helping Syd into the dress.

"NO," she said in a firm voice. "Promise you won't tell either. I love all of you dearly but, I want to let this sink all the way in before I start telling people and give them the impression I am mortified. I am quite enthused by what is growing inside of me. I just wish it were under different circumstances, you know? Can you clasp this shoe? At least these feet are still on point and not swollen."

"That is truly a blessing," she said sarcastically. "Look, Syd, I understand your feelings but, fuck what people think. This is your life, and to be honest, you are living the fuck out of it! You have done more in you mere 29 years on this earth that some people accomplish in a lifetime. You have a beautiful five bedroom, two-story, three and a half bathrooms, two car garage that you built on your own. You have your law degree and are actively and very much successfully using it. So with that being said, people should be on the lowest part of your give a fuckability scale. Seriously! "

"You are right," Syd said grabbing her and purse walking toward the door. "Forget people. They don't matter. I do!"

"Why are they always here, baby?" Shamika asked Damion pointing at Syd and Mel.

"Hell, you wanna know ask 'em?" Damion replied bluntly.

Shamika rubbed her stomach, rolled her eyes, and sucked her teeth, and said "I asked you. This yo house, ain't it? Why these other TWO females always gotta be up in our space?"

Syd overheard the conversation because of course Shamika's ghetto ass couldn't whisper worth shit, and asked Mel, "How the hell a ma'fucka gone say this YO house then turn around and say our space? Bitches stupid these days," and let out one of the loudest laughs she could.

"What she say to me in my house Damion?" Mika asked like she was about to do something.

"I said 'bitches stupid these days.' It's called subject verb agreement," Mel said laughing, pouring Syd some lemonade into a champagne glass like she just that grand.

"Why you using our dishes? We got paper cups," Shamika said trying to take the glass out of her hand.

"First of all, there is no such thing as a paper cup, and I don't do Styrofoam," Syd said drinking out of her glass, with a smile.

"Okay, Syd bring yo ass. Look who else is here!" Mel said ignoring the retard walking Syd out the back door to her favorite ex, G.

They had gone everywhere together. He picked her up and kept her up all night. He was her man and her best friend, but he wanted more than she was willing to give, and when she was ready to give it, he had already married and was trying to divorce someone else. They vowed to keep in touch because she understood… that's what she got, waiting on a man who already had someone, someone like Damion. She had learned if you love something let it go and if it comes back, it's yours. That's how you know.

"Hey, beautiful. How are you?" G said with his heavenly thick southern drawl.

"I am just fine now that I see you. How have you been Mr. Gregory Bernard Thornton?" Syd said smiling in her soul remembering their last encounter with each other, trying to pretend she hadn't seen him since before last time.

"Just fine. I've been trying to contact you for the last year or so," he said caressing her arm, catching the hint.

"Well, here I am. What's been going on in your world?" she asked with a flirtatious smile.

"I decided to focus on my career after my divorce. You revealed your heart and soul to me, gave me a chance to reflect on my decisions, and I came to the conclusion I married her for all the wrong reasons. When you and I were dating, it was mystical. But, you saw my heart aching for her and me holding on to a bitter past. By removing yourself from me and trying to be a friend, who was needed, you gave me hope and a renewed trust in love and people in general. So I need the opportunity to be a man and a friend to you. "

"Wow," Syd said with glistening, tear-filled eyes. "That is a lot to take in."

"And a lot to give at a barbeque," Mel said.

"Ugh, Mel please," Syd motioned for her to go away. "But don't go too far," she pleaded.

"Oh, what do we have here? Mr. Thornton I remember you," Alex said intruding on my beautiful moment.

"Who can forget? Alex," G said with a less than excited laugh.

"Oh, so it's like that? I know when my presence isn't appreciated," Alex said sipping his drink and going to mingle with the other guests.

"I'll be right here if you need me, honey," he rubbed Syd's back, while giving G the snake eyes.

"Look, that's really sweet and all, but I have a lot going on, and my life is kind of in shambles right now. I am stable, but unstable you get it?" Syd asked taking a big gulp of her lemonade.

"No matter what it is, we can handle it. I promise you I am ready for love and you," he said with a hopeful smile.

"Look, I am about two months pregnant, by a man who is about to marry someone else," Syd said hastily. Just as the thought escaped her lips, so did everything she'd eaten.

Mel rushed to her side to help her save face and to try to hurry and help clean up the mess. G scooped her into his arms and carried her to the restroom to clean her up. She could hear Mel behind her yelling, "Oh God!"

"I got you baby. I'm here, and it will be just fine," G said in the most reassuring voice she had ever heard.

Entering the restroom, Mel pulled her hair back and G got a cool towel and placed it on the back of her neck.

"Look, I don't know what you're expecting, but I am pretty sure this will get worse before it gets better. Thank you, but are you sure you want this?" she asked in her most sincere voice.

"Yes, all I want is you and that includes every part of you, even the parts that aren't fully developed," he said reassuring her he was there for the good, bad, and ugly.

"Are you okay, Syd?" D asked rushing into the restroom.

"You must be new pregnant. Who yo baby daddy is?" Shamika burst in.

"Ugh, damn, is anybody worried about their damn self?" Mel asked rolling her eyes.

"So, are you pregnant, Syd? Damion asked with a serious look on his face.

Making eye contact with G, Syd didn't say anything.

"Why y'all all up in her business? We bout to go. Both of y'all tripping. We're leaving," Mel said hurrying me out of the restroom.

"Thank you, Greg," Syd said, over her shoulder in an apologetic voice.

He just nodded, got up, and walked away.

Mel maneuvered through the house swiftly, grabbed her cup with one hand, and Valentino with the other. "Come on, we leaving," she said to him.

"What? We really just got here," he said slowing her down.

"Look, we got to go. My girl not feeling well," she said pointing to Syd.

"No worries," a deep caring voice said. "Stay, enjoy yourself. I'll take care of her."

Mel, turned around saying, "Who the hell are you? She ain't going with you."

Valentino stepped in, "Yea, bruh this family business."

Damion walked up is. "Everything okay? Mel what's going on?"
"WE'RE leaving," Syd said grabbing Greg's arm as he wrapped her in his arms.

"Y'all have a good evening," he said over his shoulder.

"Chryssany," Mel said.

"Syd, really?" Tino said.

"You don't even know him, and where did you come from? Who invited you?"

"Doesn't matter now. We're leaving. I'll call y'all later," Syd said getting in the car.

"What the hell is she thinking? She don't even know him like that," Damion said.

Shamika chimed in, "Why you worried? She a grown lady. She can handle herself."

D looked at her and let out a soft growl as he walked away.

"So, can we get back to the party? Damn, Mel, you so over protective," Tino said shaking his head, looking down into her eyes.

"Some people are so damn gullible. That stupid shit just happens. Fuck, I'm getting a headache. Man, I need to go," Mel said rubbing her temples.

Damion said, "So you're going to leave too, huh?"

"She should," Shamika said walking by.

"I hate that road kill, and the bitch wearing it," Mel said not lifting her head. "Where's my phone? She will call, right?" Mel said looking at Damion.

Letting out a sigh, "I hope so," he said going to look out the door noticing Alex and walking back up from the car. "You sure you want to stay? I don't think you two have run into each other, so you may want to avoid confrontation."

"What you talking about?" Tino said walking to look out the door. "Damn, you're right. Mel, let's ride. Shit, I should have stayed out the way. Y'all gone have a nigga doing hard time for some bull."

"Okay, we out D," Mel said. "If she calls you before she calls me, let me know," she said rubbing her head.

"Where to?" Tino said jumping in the driver seat of Mel's truck.

"Well first Syd's, then home. There is a bubble bath calling my name. I knew I should have hired a housekeeper, butler, maid some shit, that damn bath needs to be ready when I get there."

"Don't they have an app for that?" Tino said being funny.

"A he, he hell," Mel said side-eyeing him.

"Where the dope?" Tino said bluntly.

"Hell, I thought you knew," she said rising from her slumber.

"Nah, I ain't been in touch like that. Plus, you the one with the connects. Fuck wit me," he said not taking his eyes off the road. "She ain't here, and her nosy ass neighbors ain't even looking out. Man, I think they prejudice or something. Every time I come over the police always, 'just show up.'"

"Dude, you be walking, and look at you. Hell, I got half a mind to call the folks on yo ass, hell. You fit the profile," she said simply.

"Fuck a profile. I'm gone run up in they shit, they keep fucking with me," he said in a "get em back tone."

"And there it is, yo ass gone be locked up. They won’t let you out," she said singing. "Where the hell did she go? Damn, she stay trusting a ma fucker, everybody don't deserve yo loyalty I promise man. Damn, my head hurting again. Benson, take me home," she said snapping her finger.

"Aight, keep on," Tino said.

"But, for real take me home. My head tripping, all this shit man, damn," Mel said.

"Aight, I got you. Listen to this old school, J. E. Heartbreak." He put the music on, watched, Mel lay back, and close her eyes. He grabbed her hand and said, "She's fine, and so are you."

They drove to Mel's house to the soulful sounds. He pulled into the garage. "We're here."

"Okay," she said groggily, exiting the vehicle.

"You straight?" he asked

"Yeah, just tired as hell," she replied.

He opened the door and let her in. She walked in and coasted to her bedroom. He followed.

"Uh, what you doing? Last I checked, I wasn't your type," she said in a tired voice

"I am going to run your bath. Benson, remember?" he reminded her.

"Aw, okay, that's what's up," she said. "So when can we discuss this?"

"There's nothing to discuss. It's who I am," he said walking passed her to enter her bedroom first, and then into her bathroom he went.

"I hear ya, but," she said plopping across her bed, reaching into her night stand, "it doesn't make good sense. Is he the only person you have connected with since you been home or something?" she asked trying to put the pieces together.

"Nah, I been with a few females, but they weren't on the same thing I'm on. I'm trying to get back what I had before and get back straight. And I don't want no damn hand out. The broads I run across be scandalous and ratchet as hell."

"Sooo, he is the only one you have connected with, huh?" she said in a matter-of-fact tone. "I mean, y'all talked. You told him your plans, he actually listened, gave you advice, told you if you needed him he was there. Something like that," she said lighting her blunt.

"Yeah, how you know? You talked to him or something," he said walking out the bathroom catching the scent of her reefer. "Oh, so you the plug?" he smiled.

Mel gazed at him and saw him for what he was; a man looking for someone to accept and love him. She stared at what seemed to be his soul, six-foot-two-and-a-half-inches high, yellow, pearly white teeth, penitentiary built, hazel eyes, waves that would make you sea sick, dark black hair, with a smile that would melt your panties off. "I don't think it's him you want." she said taking a hard pull, as she got up to go into the bathroom. "Can you get that bottle of 1800 out of the mini-fridge in the corner over there? And, get my soda," she called out to him from the bathroom as she undressed.

"K, gotcha," he said getting her alcohol. "What is it you think I want and or need?" he said giggling.

"First, go get you some trifling pussy. Not that loyal 'I will be there in the morning' pussy, the kind that has a stench, a light one you, don't want the VD. Ask that trick to stick her finger in your ass while you cum," she said instructing him, settling into her bath.

"Hold up, you talking like you have experience," he said walking into the bathroom. "How you so 'informed' and why you trying to reform me? I know what I want and it ain't no trifling ass pussy," he said walking towards the tub.

"I am not trying to 'reform' you; I am trying to let you see you have an addictive personality" she said streaming the water down her arms one at a time. "So before word gets back to where you and I came from, let us try something else. And by the way, you do have me; we grew up on the same south Memphis block in a shitty ass neighborhood. I know it was hell getting out of there, but we both still have strong ties there. I know Syd and Damion have ties to the block, but they didn't grow up there WE DID. They saw the life we, lived it and got out of it. Grow up Tino and think. This shit can't leave our circle. You know the shit you have done, the people you have done it for, and the people who would love to get at you. Walk away from him, and yes I do know, I have seen this go both ways. So," she said with a stern look on her face, "question, how many women have you been with since you been out?"

"Bruh, what kind of question is that?" he said walking up on her in a defensive tone.

"Nigga you better stand the fuck down," she said not backing down. "I am still Jenny from the fucking block. You the one come in my fucking house, with yo disrespectful gay ass, talking all this sweet booty shit. Then I ask you a genuine ass question and you want to tense the fuck up," she said still calmly bathing. "Need to take all that bass out your voice before, I make ya ass a soprano. Shid, Keisha, Kim, Trina, Paris, and Christine all have been blowing me up wanting to know who you fucking, and who the new bitch is. I guess I can tell them to cut them losses because you want the dick now. So are you a top or bottom or are you a versatile bitch," she said squaring up with him.

Clinching his cheek, and through gritted teeth, he said, "Mel you need to back down, and why the fuck you still got ties to them garbage ass hoes?"

"Because just like you, I cannot fall off. They my eyes and ears in the hood. I became a lawyer for them as well as myself. That little town home in Whitehaven, what's it? She pretended to think, "The Sterling you been visiting? Yea, that bitch a welfare hoe. How you think that rent getting paid? Why you think she only has two kids by two ballers that take care of they shit? Because I made shit happen for them."

"So you think you that, bitch, huh?" he asked aggressively.

"Yep," she said rising out of the water, letting it drizzle down her body.

He froze in adoration of the way the water encircles her supple breasts, trickling down her areola, to slowly drip off her nipple. The way the water ran down her thick voluptuous legs as she raised one then the other with each foot pointed. On her left foot a tattooed anklet reached her perfectly pedicure toes. *What I wouldn't give to be just that tattoo,* he thought, *the tip of the key would be just fine. Her ass, so round and juicy, just to squeeze it a little and a small tap, would do me just fine,* he pictured in his mind.

"T, the towel," she demanded.

"Yeah, hurry up and cover up," he said with a bit of urgency in his voice.

"What, am I making you timid or uncomfortable?" she said bending over to dry her legs, purposely positioning her ass in his direction.

He grabbed his dick, and licked his lips.

She stood and walked towards him, "I thought you wanted something I couldn't give you."

"Look, stop playing," he demanded.

"Why?" she said grabbing his member and slightly gripping it. "Let me show you what you been missing." She walked out of the bathroom, entirely nude, and laid full spread on the bed.

"Mel, stop fucking with me. Don't do shit you might regret in the morning," he said hoping she was serious.

I" know exactly what I'm doing," she said rolling over to expose her freshly waxed, phat, and waiting pussy. "Come sit by me," she said. "Now, after all these years, I know you ain't scared are you?"

"Scared of what?" he said frozen in place.

"Oh, that's cool. I like taking control," she said standing again, walking towards him.

Again he was frozen, looking at her coke bottle shape and hour glass ass. *Damn, this can't be real* he thought.

She approached him and began to undress him. "This is okay, right?" she asked slipping his T-shirt over his head.

"Yeah," he breathe out.

"Great, then come out them jeans, shoes, and all that," she coaxed as she walked over to get a new blunt, lit it, and watched him undress. "Come here, sit down," she motioned for him to sit on the bed.

He did as he was told, fully naked and rock hard. He sat on the side of the bed unsure of what was about to happen.

She mounted him, "Are you sure you're ready for this?" she asked.

He shook his head as he slipped inside, "Damn, it's tight," he moaned out.

"God damn, this won't work," she said backing off of him.

"Yes, it will," T stood and reaching out to her. He grabbed her and wrapped his arms around her waist. "You done started something now." Staring into her eyes, he planted kisses all over her face, slow and soft, in a clockwise motion, skipping her lips, then back to her forehead, a tiny peck on her nose, and a massive kiss, where she gripped his tongue, and sucked it, making him moan out in pleasure, and she could feel his dick throbbing. "Lie down. I won't hurt you, I promise," he said still looking her in her eyes, flashing that million dollar smile.

"Okay, but give me a sec to get used to it, then I'm back in control," she agreed.

"Aight," he shook his head, still in awe at the fact that this was happening.

He helped her onto the bed and lie her tenderly there. As he mounted her, she squealed out in pleasure. He kissed her neck with juicy wet kisses, and spelled his name over her heart, and he began his decent, only stopping to visit each breast for a small kiss, tug, and a slight nibble. His mouth watered and the excitement built, just anticipating how she would taste. He placed the tip of his tongue on her clitoris only to get a small taste.

She moaned out in delight, "Wait, I can't."

He began kissing her pearl, deep and with a slight suck she exploded all over his chest as he raised his head just in time. "Do it again," he begged, as he slipped his pointer and index finger in and kissed deeper than before and began humming.

Once more she exploded.

"You ready?" he said coming back up to meet her eyes, and combine their souls.

He entered her slowly, while kissing her delicately. "How's that?" he asked not wanting to hurt her.

"Mmmmm," she moaned. "Damn it, I been waiting a long time for this." He pushed in a little more. "Oh, my," she said. "Wait, it's too much." He backed out a little and started slow stroking, easing his way in a little at a time.

He growled trying to hold his nut. "I can't take it, and it's too good."

"Let it out," she said as she gripped his back enjoying the pain and pleasure.

She commenced to gripping him from the inside. He yelled out, "Mel, wait," and exploded into her body as she exploded all over him. He lay down beside her and they both fell into a deep sleep.

Mel awakened to find herself alone. She got up and walked around. "T?" she yelled through the house. "Damn, I guess, it was just for the moment," she thought as she walked back into her bedroom. She went back into her room, went into the bathroom and showered. And, back to bed she went, trying not to think about what had just happened to her.

He came in quietly so as not to wake her, placing rose petals throughout her bedroom, gently placing a well-written letter and a card on her nightstand.

Now, it's time to wake her, he thought, as he began kissing her lower lips, slowly as if he had missed her and was making up for all the past years, until she squirted all over his chin and down his chest. He came up. "Good morning sleepy head," he said as he entered slowly while kissing her deep and passionately, where it makes her wonder "where have you been all my life."

"Where were you? Where did you go," she asked trying to figure out what happened.

"I had to get something to show you how appreciated you are while slow stroking, and allowing her to feel every inch of you. You don't know what having you around means to me," he whispered. "I have loved you forever. Thank you."

"It's my turn to thank you," Mel said pushing him off her, noticing the roses she smiled and kissed him deeply as she attempted to move down his body.

He tapped her round perky ass to say, "No bring that pussy here." She followed his instructions as she began slowly caressing his penis with her mouth. She opened wide to allow as much as she could possibly could, no gag reflex, permitted the saliva to run down the shaft and she continued to swallow him. He wrapped his arms around her hips in pleasure. Not to be shown up, he began to tongue fuck her, slowly. As his tongue entered her, he allowed the juices to flow out of his mouth on to the sheets. As his tongue came out, he hummed with that baritone depth, making her body shiver in delight, with a light pop of the lips she began to explode. T turned them over to allow him better access to her and so he could fuck her throat and he slow stroked her mouth. She moaned out in pleasure again, releasing another powerful squirt. He wanted to catch it all in his mouth. As he slowly inserted his pointer finger in her ass, she yelled out, "Ooooohhhhh, yes, do it in there," she said to him.

Again repositioning, them T turned around to make eye contact with Mel, and asked, "May I?" as he began kissing her to taste each other's juices from their lips.

She pushed him back, to a standing position. As she closely followed, she turned her back still standing, and bent over grabbing the back of her knees, he slowly entered her ass carefully not to hurt her. She squirted and moaned out in pleasure, "Yeah, just like that. Go slow."

"I got you babe," he said trying to hold it together. Their rhythms synced as he stroked in, she threw it back, and tightened up as he drew out. He began to moan loudly as he grabbed her hips. She stood, reached behind her to grip his neck as he came, his knees buckled. "Damn, girl," he said out of breathe.

"I won't fall asleep because you may leave again," she said walking into her bathroom.

"Wait, let me," he said barely getting off the floor.

She turned the light on to reveal more rose petals, two wine glasses, a bottle of Pinot Noir, because he remembered it was her favorite. She walked in to see in her tub were bath rose petals and little rose fizzies.

"Push the button, baby girl. It's bath time, right?" he asked as he walked in behind her.

"When did you do all of this? I know I wasn't sleeping this hard," she said.

"The first time you woke up, I had just gotten back, so I jumped in the pantry so you wouldn't ruin the surprise. I apologize for allowing you to think you were just for the moment."

"No worries. You are here now," she said pressing the button to run her bath at her perfect temp. She got in and let the water run as she sat there,

He entered the tub opposite her, saying, "I don't know what I was thinking with Alex. I mean, I guess it was just because he was there and listened when no one else had time. I was in a fucked up place and couldn't shake it. All y'all was doing what y'all do, and there I was fucked up, broke, lonely. Hell, I couldn't even hustle. My hoes was tied up or tied down to a square ass nigga, so shit, he was there and listened and fucked with me, tough."

"Well, how you feeling now?" Mel asked trying to make sure it wasn't just for the day. "And why wouldn't you reach out to one of us. You were living with Syd. Hell, she ain't never at home. Why you call somebody, like me? I been yo A1 since day one... I'm slick offended now that you didn't .What the fuck? How? Why…."

He grabbed her face and kissed her. "I didn't know baby. Now I do. I see you. I see you for real. You loyal even when I wasn't. I'm sorry for all the shit I started," he looked in her eyes. "I'm sorry for being an ass," he said wrapping his hand around her neck gently. He starts to message her neck. He moved her head tenderly as he took a juicy, wet, bite out of the side of her neck. She moaned in pleasure. Please let me make it up to you," he gripped her neck a little tighter. She moaned again. "Tell me you love me," he said slipping his free hand into the water to find her secret place. He slightly flicked her clitoris, while nibbling her neck. She laid back to allow him access to her neck and breasts. He grinned and winked as he slipped his finger inside. He licked between her supple breasts, up to her neck, then her lips. As their lips met, she grasped him as if he were running from her. She breathed in his bottom lip. He returned her soft careful kiss. He began kissing down to her breasts. The right, one he bit and sucked through kisses. Her nipple seemed to pulsate to his heartbeat; he licked it like ice cream, slow from the bottom to the top, with his kisses gently placing the cherry on top. He brought his finger to her lips to give her a taste of his new found love, her juices. He placed deep, meticulous kisses on her lips, to taste her, while enjoying the sweet taste of her kisses. Then, he stood over her, as she took him into her mouth as if he were her air. Leaning her head back, she gave him all access to her throat, where he gently thrust deep and moaned "Ooooooohhhh, shit girl. Damn," he said through thick heavy breathes. She then began contracting her throat muscles to mimic her vagina gripping his manhood, as she carefully sucked, not wanting to leave a piece of his dick out. She then massaged his balls, while gentle but aggressively massaging his perineum. He emptied into her mouth as she sat up to swallow every drop. He collapse back into the tub, while she stood allowing the water to drip from her soaking wet body. She then stepped out and bent over to pick up her towel. He took the opportunity to return the favor. Leaning over the edge of the tub, he kissed her lips; making her moan out in pleasure. He stepped out of the tub, kneeling down with her still bent over in front of him. He grabbed her thighs to restrain her movement. He again kissed her and sucked her clitoris, while sliding a finger into her ass; she squealed with pleasure, as she squirted all over his face. He started vigorously sucking and fingering her ass. She ached and screamed in pleasure as she fell to her knees. With her on all fours, he entered from the back, "How that dick feel?" he asked as he slid in. No, words could escape her lips; her mind has gone to erotic ecstasy. He gently pushed in and slowly pulled out to allow her every inch of pleasure. He spit in the crack of her ass, just before circling her anus with his ring finger. Tears formed in her eyes as he slipped his finger into her ass, while slowly stroking deep inside her. Her body began to tense up on his dick as she squirted out of control. Feeling her body tightened around him, he released what little he had left. "Damn, girl where did that come from?" he asked; again, no response. "Mel?" he said rolling her limp body over. "Mel?" he said. Her eyes were open, but unfocused. "What's wrong with you? Wake up. Talk to me. Mel....."

Mel began to speak indistinctively, still her body had no movement, nor was her gaze focused.

"What are you saying? What's going on? Are you hurt? Is this normal? Did I break you?" Valentino asked truly concerned for her.

Becoming more audible, she spoke, "Damn, baby boy, that was my shit," as she smiled rolled over and fell fast asleep.

The Mall

I had to find me a new best friend. It seemed as if your work had taken the place of people. You never even called to just joke around anymore," Damion explained. "We used to laugh and chill all the time in college. You went to law school and buckled down and threw me to the side. I thought maybe you would come around and love me again, and we would be together, but no, you decided to keep the real estate office and do the law thing, but what about me? Syd, what about us?" he said walking towards her. "And now this and us, and here we are, and I don't know. I can't apologize anymore for the past or the present. I can only say could've, would've, should've..." he said looking in her eyes.

"Could've, would've, should've, huh?" she repeated to him. "Well now, thanks,"she said removing herself from his gaze. "I think you should leave. Sometimes it's best to leave well enough alone. Why did you come to visit me today? Like what was your overall purpose?" she asked with her arms folded as her head tilted with a confused look on her face wondering exactly how hurt she should feel or confused or even if she should feel anything at all.

"I came to explain to you that I love you, and I am still in love with you, but I am not going to play this back and forth game with you Syd," he said containing what seemed to be rage in his eyes. "Look, you act like I am just here on a humbug; I am pouring my heart to you and trying to be open and honest with you…"

"Pouring your heart? Please!" she said unfolding her arms and throwing her hand up in his face. "You have the nerve to come to my home after the ordeal that took place at yours, with your house mate, who which might I add, has been less than tolerable, threatens me on a regular basis. Then you let me know 'you aren't about to play this back and forth game with me?' What the heck? You double minded, egotistical, self-centered, maniac!" She paced through the kitchen trying to stay calm. "Back in college you had your fair share of 'Shamikas' when I was in law school. You told me you had gotten chlamydia from some random chic at a pool hall in the restroom. So of course I backed off. You were sticking your Johnson in every Jane, Jill, and Jasmine that smiled at you. Even when we did actually date, do you remember Mallory and the pregnancy scare freshman year? Yeah, or the pictures you couldn't help but send, or the videos of the two of you that you swore were you and I? I've gotten waxed on a regular basis since senior year you douche bag! And I let that all slide," she said pantomiming safe as if she were an umpire at a baseball game. "Or yes, what about Kendall the huge chic that kicked a dent in your car in front of my parents' home while we were visiting from college?" she said now speaking just above a whisper trying to control her tone. "SO, don't give me grief about this crap. As a matter of fact, get out. It's too early for this BS. You and that trash belong together," she said huffing, pushing him out toward the door. "You don't deserve me. You don't deserve my anger. You don't deserve my happiness, and frankly you don't deserve my friendship. So you made your freaking choice, so suck it up and live with it," she said as they reached her front door. "Good riddance," she said as she slammed the door and washed her hands of him and that situations. She slowly walked back into her kitchen, trying to catch her breath and not have a seizure. "Please Jesus, I am okay," she whispered to herself to calm down. She rubbed her baby bump. "We are going to be just fine. One less nuisance," she said still pacing.

"Are you okay, Syd?" Shawn asked as he walked down her kitchen steps.

"I'm fine, just getting a little water," she attempted to lie as the sweat beads still filled her nose.

"I heard everything, baby girl," he said honestly walking toward her now. "Are you okay?" he grabbed her shoulders and looked her in her eyes.

"Yes and no." The tears began to fill her eyes, but no other words escaped.

"Now, you listen, and you listen good, when a person shows you they don't give a fuck about you, fucking listen! Certain things people and places aren't meant I mean they aren't in our story. So be damn sure that a person has your best interest before you go investing your time, talents, and tissues. People will use you for whatever they need. Most people think it's just money or material things, but people will use you for the emotional connection because they fucked up with the person they think is the one. Or sex because they are horny, and can't get it from the person that they love, so they will say anything before, during, and after. You have to pray for discernment so the right people will stay and the wrong people will walk away. I love you and I am not trying to hurt you, but you need to know, the way you jump from man to man, bed to bed shows me you want love. When you leave as quickly as you came, it means you can't commit. You were looking for momentary satisfaction, not a real relationship or connection. Love is not a toy, and there are men out here that love you and want nothing but what's best for you, and there are those who just enjoy banging you because of the passion. I love you, will probably never bang you, but that's a whole other story." He laughed and moved closer to her. "You need to be prepared for what's about to happen whoever your child's father is, I am positive you know exactly who he is and just don't know how he will handle it." Placing his hand around her waist he said, "You have to just pay attention, boo. This hurt you keep going through isn't fair to you or any of us who have to watch you suffer through it. Wake up. See life how it truly is, and stop walking alone. There is a God who is waiting for you to ask, so do that and watch Him work. I know we rarely get to talk without everyone around, so if I never say anything else, hear this now." Shawn ended his lecture as Alex walked into the kitchen. "Morning handsome."

"Morning cutie, uh what's the T, boo?" Alex said making contact with the hurt in her eyes. "Ugh, look Miss Bitch, you need to get your shit together. This sad shit ain't you," he said walking past Shawn, giving him the evil eye. "I don't know what you and Mister Man just discussed, but my bitch too flawless for this shit. Okay," he said grabbing her hands, literally lifting her from her oak and cream accented kitchen chair. "Get it together. I didn't stay for *All My Children* heffa. I stayed *for Real Housewives*, so amp it up. Go get dressed." He spun her in 180 degrees by the shoulders. "We going shopping. Where the keys at boo?" Alex glanced over his shoulder asking Shawn.

"I'll be ready in two shakes," he said galloping up the hide away staircase off the side of the kitchen.

"Yasss," Alex exclaimed. "Let's get it, bitches."

"I'm ready; he ready, what you doing Syd?" Alex asked bursting into her bedroom.

"Well, none of my bottoms fit. I can't buckle with this belly. I mean, I can," she said lifting her shirt and showing him how her used to be oh-so-sexy pants looked like they're oh-so-small.

"Um no, wearing clothes this tight gone make the baby come out with three and a half toes, four fingers, no hair and crossed eyed. Hell, I am suffocating just looking at this," he said grabbing her zipper and unbuttoning the jeans. "This will be therapy for little Alex, too," he said motioning for her to take the pants off as he walked into the closet.

"Who is little Alex?" she said still a little tickled and a little offended by his previous comments.

"Don't play. That's our baby's name," he said parting her clothes in the closet without even looking up. "It fits both genders, so it's only right that the little one be named that. Hell, even if you don't, I am already planning on calling my little boo Alex." he said matter of factly as he threw a black "supposedly'" fitted dress with nude floral print accents and quarter length sleeves in her direction. "Put that on," he said again not looking up.

"I can't fit in this, which is why I have never worn it," she said holding the dress up in disbelief.

"Shawn, honey, she needs help", Alex instructed Shawn.

Shawn approached her and mouthed, "I'm sorry. Before saying, "Okay, babe," to Alex.

"Arms up," he said as he tapped her sides. She put her arms up and he removed her shirt and replaced it with the dress and stood back. "Babe, you're right," he said as he stepped back and examined her new appearance.

Alex resurfaced from the closet. "This is the dress you used to not fit, honey I am enjoying you with curves. Little Alex is putting some meat on that po' ass in all the right places. I hope you keep it, honey," he said handing her a pair of black six inch open wedged heels. Shawn approached again, kneeled, and helped her put on the shoes, even latched the ankle straps. "This is giving me life, honey. Turn," Alex said as he twirled his finger. "I love it. Go look. You will, too."

Speechless, she walked into her closet and stood in front of a full length mirror, and to her surprise, she loved it, too. The belly was perfectly shown, not too tight where her clothes looked too small, or to large where it seems as though she were trying to hide it. She no longer had a lil "tooty booty" as Alex always teased. She was perfectly stacked like a brick house, hips and all. "Thank you, Baby Alex," she whispered and rubbed her belly, took a final glance winked at herself, and walked out. "Okay, I love it. Needs a little of this and that," she said walking to across the room to her vanity searching for her three strand pearls, bracelet, and earrings.

"I am so glad you got this mane, pressed because this wrap is where it's at with this dress," he said untying her hair and combing it down.

"I love you, Alex. Thank you," she said feeling sentimental.

"Oh, don't thank me until after the shopping trip," he said waving her words off then bending down to embrace her. He caught a glimpse of them in the mirror and said, "Yes, this is selfie worthy," taking his phone out as she hastily applied her eye shadow, liner, and mascara.

"Oh, I need some of that." He picked up her mascara and touched up his lashes.

"Ready, boo?" *Snap, flash, snap.*

Through the flashes and snaps the horn blew. "Is Shawn outside?" she asked looking around.

"Yes, he got the car, your car. It has the most trunk space," he said laughing motioning for her to come on.

Shawn dropped them off at the door and parked as they went in and made their route through the Wolfchase.

Shawn met them at their first stop, the food court. Syd hated the smell of the Chinese food here but she couldn't wait to get a deep fried anything.

"Okay, so let's hit a couple stores," Alex said more excited than a child in a candy store.

"Okay, let's," Syd agreed, seemingly just as anxious. "Should we wait for Shawn?" Syd asked looking back wondering where could he be.

"Chile he ain't new to this. When he comes in, we both will get a text or a call and he will come to us," Alex said not looking back ready to shop. "Oooh, Pandora! Let's bookmark this journey through pregnancy." In he went with Syd attached. "Okay, let's pick out your trinkets." He began picking random charms, while Syd looked around for Shawn. As she began her search for trinkets and charms their phones buzzed, Alex, quickly responded, "Pandora," and continued his journey.

Shawn walked in. "How does this enhance your wardrobe, exactly?" in a playful tone.

"Honey, I don't know, but I am sure glad he's having a ball," Syd replied eyeing Alex as he finished up their bracelets.

"Okay, Motherhood Maternity. Up the elevator and to the right," Alex said with no hesitation as he led the way out of the store prancing, leading the way.

"Um, excuse me, how do you know that? And follow up, if I may, location assistance really?" Syd said confused and surprised.

"Oh, honey," he said hitting the elevator button, "I Googled on the ride here while you daydreamed about whatever you and D were arguing about this morning."

"Alex," Syd said looking as if he had betrayed her trust.

Alex held his hands in an "I surrender position." "I didn't say anything hon, I promise."

"Oh, he didn't hon. I know math; I saw his car pulling out of the drive this morning, and when I came down and saw the distraught look on your face, it all added up." They exited the elevator and walked a few stores down.

"Here's BEBE," Syd said wanting to stop in.

"Yeah, there it went. Once these few months pass, we will come and revisit, but as for right now, um, Motherhood suites you, sorry boo," Alex said grabbing her arm and speed walking past.

Syd felt a little sad as they walked into the maternity store. "Okay, so is it labeled by weight, by months, by inches, or…." she said in an exasperated tone.

"No, ma'am. We are here to guide you through the journey of shopping here today. These are regular, sizes ma'am," the clerk said smiling eerily. "My name is Joslyn, and whatever you need let me know," she smiled.

"Oh okay, honey. Well, I like this for her, and I want to know what size she needs for now and what she will need in the near future in the event I come alone to get her something."

"Oh, wow, most fathers aren't that attentive. You're lucky," Joslyn said with a smirk.

"You know she is. I tell her all the time, if he and I were ever to become homosexuals he'd be all mine," Shawn said seeing her sarcasm and one upping her.

"Oh, okay," the clerk said. "Well, if you don't mind me asking how many months are you, and may I measure your belly. Was it an all of a sudden or did you gradually grow into your baby bump?" she asked.

"Oh well, um… I am two months now, and it was a gradual bump. Are there any invasive questions I may have missed?" Syd said smiling briskly.

"Oh, no ma'am, we have ask those questions to kind of estimate where you will be as the gentleman asked about your future months. I will be right back with a chart seems that I may have forgotten it."

"I'll go with you," Alex said. "That way we can gather options as we return."

"What's going on, honey? Are you okay?" Shawn asked walking around Syd to look in her eyes. "What just happened?"

"Look, I don't like people asking questions about my child, ANYTHING about my child. She's not my doctor and that's my personal business," Syd said defensively.

"Okay, well first calm down. She was doing her job. You still want to look a certain way when you are out in public, and it has to fit for you and baby Alex, so calm down and take it with a grain of salt 'k?" Shawn explained.

"Baby Alex, huh? You, too?" Syd smiled. "Okay, you guys are something else."

"Yeah, we know. Well, from what I hear, that's just yo baby daddy," he said smiling with his mouth and eyes tremendously amused.

"Oh, my you are so silly," she said trying to contain her giggle.

"Okay, so here are some options I picked out," Alex said with two arms full of clothes.

"That's nice, so we know I can or will wear these at some point during the pregnancy?" Syd asked.

"Honey, you are about to try most of this on. No worries, we will wait though," he said smiling.

"Ugh, Alex, so much. Okay, let's get started," Syd said, grabbing an olive green long line, round neck, dress. As she slipped it on, she liked the way the belt sat right above her bump. She smiled then was immediately sadden by all the possibilities of what could be.

"Are you okay in there?" Alex said.

"Yeah, just finishing up," she said composing herself. She stepped out and felt like she was on the red carpet.

"Boo, you look, great. Now this," he said handing her another dress. They continued trying on dresses for the better part of two hours. "You are all belly, ass, and hips.

I love it," he said as she came out of the dressing room with her original outfit on.

"I could really go for a nap or a coffee," Syd said feeling more tired than usual as they walked to the counter. "We'll take all of it." She handed the clerk her card and turned. "What are we eating when we leave here? I don't want mall food, anymore?"

"Ma'am you don't want the total? These clothes aren't the cheapest, and you have a lot of 'em," the cashier said.

"Excuse me?" Syd said trying to follow the question.

"Well, you racked up. You've been in here trying on, and now you have a card that you didn't even ask for the price. I mean, I'm just saying," the cashier said in a leisure tone.

"Because it is all there. I am confident in that fact, and passed that, I wouldn't buy a car without a test drive. Seeing as though this is the only pregnancy I have experienced, I want to do it right and get exactly what I need. I made great career decisions which allow me to never have to ask how much, so please swipe the card before you lose a sale. Thank you. Oh, and here is my ID before you ask", Syd said irritated by what seemed like allegations.

"Here you are, ma'am," the clerk said, handing her, her ID back.

"Where is your supervisor?" Alex said in a deep and louder than conversational tone.

"Is there a problem?" an older lady rushed over and asked.

"Yes, your cashier seems to believe that my wife can't afford her purchase, and has taken too long trying on her items," Shawn stepped up and explained.

"I'm sure there must be a misunderstanding," the manger explained looking passed them and at the cashier.

"Yes, I'm sure. Babe, are you sure you want to patronize these people?" Shawn said looking at the attendants as though they weren't there.

"Yes, my time is just as precious as theirs, and I have spent too much of it here to have it be a waste", Syd explained. "Please have your cashier to take a few more classes in economics. I would not have come in wasting your and my time to try on, walk to the counter, and have her to scan just to hand her a card that may decline. Where's Joslyn? She was a great help," Syd asked the manager

"You know, she's don, Are those all our bags? Thank you. We won't come here again," Shawn said grabbing most of the bags.

"Maybe its skin tone," Alex said over his shoulder as he grabbed the last bag.

"Wow, I can't believe that experience. Won't go back there. Seriously at all," Syd said as they walked down to the escalator.

"Oh, look, there's Damion," Alex said pointing below the escalator.

"Where is that damn Damion at?" Alex said louder than Syd's ears cared to hear.

And with that, Shamika's big ass mouth said, "Uh who is that with the ghetto ass?" as Damion made eye contact with Alex.

"I got yo ghetto right here, Miss thang," Alex said in an all too real tone.

"Oh Alex, it's you," she responded in a less than delighted tone. "Babe your friends are like roaches. They're everywhere."

"You would know, wouldn't you?" Syd chimed in.

"Oh, sweetie you finally got a perm, I knew it was to comb when it was balled up, but the baby must've took that to a new level," she said chuckling

"No, actually it isn't a perm," Shawn said in a tired of this shit breathe.

"Oh, a sew in? You need to give me her number, she did good, especially with what you got to work with," Shamika said pointing at Syd's hair.

"No, Miss Ratchet, it's her hair straight. Something you obviously ain't too familiar with," Alex said reading the hood rat. "Damn, D you quiet. Cat got yo tongue?" he said cutting his eyes." I've never been pussy whipped, but I imagine this is it, in the rarest of form."

"NO, we're shopping for the baby," Damion said through gritted teeth.

"What's that vein in your neck? Seems to be pulsating. You should really try to relax," Syd said smiling.

"Are you guys on a shopping trip," Damion said ignoring Syd and only talking to Shawn and Alex.

"No, we're shopping for our baby, too," Alex said rubbing Syd's little belly.

"Oh, poor thing. It must be tough not knowing who yo baby daddy is. Me and mine have to go, though. Something over here is making me sick," Shamika said pulling Damion away from them.

"Could be that fugly ass attitude, but can't forget you brought that with you," Alex said waving her off. "I hate that, hole in the wall ass bitch. She makes my goddamn ass hurt, ugh. But she did say something. When do we meet the man who got you all knocked up?" Alex looked Syd square in the eye.

"Oh, um is that my phone?" Syd said picking up her pace towards the ladies' room.

"What's the T honey?" Alex said keeping up. You normally tell me everything. Unless you don't know," he said with a slight giggle.

She looked at him and just tried to walk away. "Shawn, can we go please?"

"We need to talk about this," Alex said not stopping.

Shawn agreed, not even going toward an exit.

"Hello, hello? Oh, hey, yeah I'm at the Wolfchase with Alex and Shawn," she said fighting the tears.

"Your phone was really ringing? Best timing ever," Alex thought aloud.

"Would you please?" she said as the tears began to fall. She dashed to the ladies' room to try and clear her head and stop the tears. *Syd, get it together. It's fine. You're fine* she said to herself in the mirror. *Pleeeeeaaaaassssseeee calm down.* She took solid deep breathes which only made it worse because she was in a public restroom. Her phone rang again. "I'm right here with Shawn and Alex. I'll be right out," she chimed.

"So, you're leaving, with him? Alex asked.

"What about our talk? What about what needs to be discussed?" Shawn asked.

Damion made eye contact with Syd from across the mall and saw G standing there holding her hand and stroking her hair. His face filled with sorrow and he turned away.

"Okay, we're leaving," Syd said taking charge of a very confusing situation.

G

"So, where to beautiful?" he asked Syd with those gorgeous crystal clear unwavering truthful eyes.

"Anywhere you feel the need to take me," Syd said astonished by all the times he has swooped in to save her without question. "I have a question for you," she said as she tapped his shoulder.

"Yes, whatever it is," he said without turning around.

She began to giggle, but felt more than giggle coming up. "Oh, my," she breathed out as she opened her door and let go off what seemed like all the food that she had just recently devoured.

"Are you okay?" he reached over pulling her hair back.

"Yes, I'm fine," she said readjusting herself in the passenger seat. "Thank you for saving me; you don't know how much I appreciate you right now, and before you didn't even make notice of seeing me and just doing what you did, no questions asked. Wow, Thank you."

"No worries, baby girl, but are you going to tell me what's going on? We have spent some time together recently, and this 'illness' has been relevant. So please clue me in, I love you and I am not going anywhere, and you know I don't scare easily. Talk to me, queen."

"Well, I didn't want to tell you because I didn't know how you would react, but I am pregnant and my child's father isn't and will never be in the picture. So, if you want, you can just take me home. I can take care of myself," Syd said in a no-nonsense tone.

"Okay, I will take you home," he said while turning the music up to drown out any more words she may utter.

She thought to herself, *Man I really messed this up terribly. Oh, well, maybe it isn't meant for me to be with him or anyone*. She laid her head back, trying to get her thoughts together as they rode. She found herself drifting off to sleep, thinking she didn't think she lived this far out. Finally, she rose up to take a look around. They were pulling into his driveway.

"Honey, we're home," he said, leaning over to unbuckle her seatbelt.

She smiled and said, "This is so unexpected. Where did you come from?" gazing at a true to life angel. "I definitely didn't want to go home where they would all come and ask they're questions."

"I came from a wonderful place, where you left me. That's why I knew God sent me here to you at this moment to do for you."

She sat in amazement until her door opened. Again, there he stood waiting for her. "This has to be a dream or something. Jesus, don't let me wake up."

"Are you coming in, or did you seriously want me to take you home?" he said with an embarrassed look on his face.

"No, not at all. To be honest, I thought, that's where we were going, and you were done with me all together this time," she said sharing in his embarrassment.

He scooped her up into his arms and said, "Oh, no babe. It's you and I until the end of time, just so you know," he winked as he carried her into his home.

"I am always amazed when entering this place. It's heavenly and soothes my inner self. Man, it brings back memories seeing this place again," she said as her feet finally touched his signature marbled floor.

"So, you want to bathe? I will get that ready for you," he said walking upstairs. Looking back, noticing she hadn't moved he said, "Are you okay, sweetie?" turning and walking back in her direction. "Do you need anything?"

"No, just our moments are all I need," she said wanting to kiss him. "But I will take that bath and a toothbrush please," she said as she took the lead up his right staircase.

"Yeah, I will do you one better," he said coming up behind her and lifting her up the stairs.

"Okay, how about a 360 shower?" she said reaching the top.

"Are you sure? Wouldn't want to get the beautiful, soft, flowing, wrap wet," he said half smiling, gently placing her down turning her to face him.

"Oh, whatever. I hope to never have to go back. I want to become a hermit here with you. No one knows where I am or where I will be. I don't care about this hair," she said running her fingers through it. "I don't care about these clothes," she said as she began to undress.

"Hey, you just wait one moment," he said stopping her in her moment of clarity.

"What? Is there someone here?" she asked covering her breasts.

"Nope, I just have always wondered why you never cover your vagina and cover your breasts," he said smiling as his eyes slightly closed, and he covered his mouth trying to shield his expression.

"Wow, why would you do that?" she turned and walked toward his master bedroom. "I'm going to shower and to wash almost all my problems away."

"Okay, cutie I love this view. Did you want something else to eat? I recovered your soul from the vomit in the parking lot," he said pretending to hold it in his hand.

Smiling she turned ,still walking and said, "I was feeling a bit soulless thank you, AND I could actually go for some ice cream and ginger ale, please."

"Coming right up," he said bowing to her. "Anything else?" he said with his head still to the floor.

She stopped at the door, "Yes!"

He stood, "And what might that be?"

"Don't go too far," she winked and walked into the room.

"I will always be right where you need me to be; remember that," he whispered.

Syd walked through his room as if she were in a museum, admiring all the beautiful novelties, also reminiscing about all the memories of them being big kids. "This man, this man, he can't be real," she thought aloud. She looked over his California king bed and saw them jumping in the bed and having pillow fights, where the pillows burst open. She gazed at the space between the bed and his sliding door, beside the fireplace, where they had dance battles and karaoke sing offs. Her eyes began to fill with tears, remembering how their Christmas plans were ruined when his ex-wife decided to pull him in. He called her Christmas Eve in a low sad voice plainly stating, "MY WIFE and I are working through our issues and so we can no longer have contact. We decided divorce wasn't the best option," and just disconnecting the line. He later apologized and explained how things hadn't worked out how they had thought they would. She shook herself back to reality and walked into his master bath, where when she stepped in, the floor automatically began to heat; she walked passed his sauna, again reminisced while looking at his garden style whirlpool and remembered the nights spent and the bubble bath fights, that ended in kisses and so much more. She looked in his mirror at how time had changed her. She rubbed her baby bump and mouthed, ""I love you already. She continued her journey into his shower where she set the temperature, turned the water on, pulled her now straight hair up, and out of her face, tied it into a bun, and stepped in. She let the water run over her face, down her neck, over her breasts, wrap around her belly, down her legs, in between her toes and down the drain. She opened her eyes to look for body wash because she always admired his scent, and to her surprise, he remembered; Love Spell by Victoria's Secret was waiting there for her. She smiled at the bottle and shook her head. She began to lather herself with what she thought was her favorite and began to gag, NO, no, no, what is this, she said aloud in a grotesque voice.

"Babe, what's going on?" he said running in to aid her.

"I don't know," she said still gagging, trying to understand why this was happening.

"Have you been using this kind of soap or not," he asked.

"No, I've been using Caress. Why?" she asked trying to get it off her as soon as she could. She grabbed his body wash and poured more than normal in her hand and lathered it all over.

He looked at her confused. "What are you doing?"

"I love this stuff," she said. "I guess it loves me back," she smiled.

He shook his head, chuckled, and walked away. "I'm glad that works for you," he said over his shoulder.

"Excuse me, I need a towel. I forgot to get one," she said as she turned the shower on from all directions.

"Okay", he said detouring to his linen closet. He reached in, grabbed a mint green, billowy, towel that was purchased with her in mind. He smiled as he handed it to her.

"Oh, thank you," she said not really noticing the details of the towel. She wiped her face, and cleared her eyes, and took a good look at the towel. "Really?" she said looking at him suspiciously.

"What?" he said as if he were oblivious as to what she was speaking of as he turned around to walk away.

"You know what," she said, walking behind him with the biggest smile on her face. She rounded the corner seeing the big bowl of butter pecan and mint chocolate chip ice cream on his bed. "How do you remember so much?" she asked aloud never taking her eyes off the ice cream.

"When we were creating our moments, it seemed as if time stood still. Even when I was still straddling the line," he said twisting his hand in a back and forth motion, feeling a bit awkward.

"Okay, yeah, well, ice cream," she said in a cookie monster voice. "May I have a T-shirt, please?" she smiled looking over her shoulder.

“Sure.” He reached over behind her. Lying on the bed was a white V-neck T –shirt already waiting for her.

“Oh, so you think you know me huh?” she questioned as she pulled the shirt over her head?

“Nope,” he said as he plopped down on the bed, “but I knew you wouldn’t lie around in that towel. So… you’re welcome,” He smiled looking up at her.

“She reexamined her bowl, wait two spoons? I am not sharing with you!” she said picking it up.

“Nope, I’m sharing with you,” he said gently picking up one of the spoons.

“Oh, well in that case,” she said smiling getting comfortable.

“So, tell me why you want to be a hermit? You have never wanted to be to yourself. You have always been a people person, and you never get enough of your extended family," he asked genuinely concerned.

"Sometimes, I just want to give up, ya know?" she said taking a spoonful of ice cream. "Like, why have I worked so hard to become what I am? I started my real estate career just before college, literally the summer before. Yes, it was a tough journey, but I made it," another spoonful of ice cream. "I mean long nights of studying, long days in some office trying to sell properties and for what? To become someone's baby's momma? I mean this truly cannot be it for me," she said giving in to her insecurities and her emotions as her tears fell.

"Well," he repositioned himself behind her, removing the bowl and placing it on the night stand, "you're not just a BABY MOMMA. You are so much more. Look at what you have accomplished. This kid gets the best of you and you should be proud of that."

"I am just so tired of always being the one having to be strong, to keep the secrets, to just be seemingly weak so they can be strong. I am just tired point blank, period. I keep asking God and seeking out answer as to what to do, but nothing seems to come about. I don't know what to do."

"I have all the energy you need and am willing to share it with you," he said with her still calmly nestled in his arms. "Namaste, I love you," he whispered. "Remember, it's always darkest just before light, and understand if you keep going through the e situations you're not learning what you need to. Sometimes we have to take a step back and look at our storm to know exactly what's causing it. I know you were just talking, but the warrior spirit you have won't allow you to give up. God has you and allowed the Devil to place that thought just to test you; he's still holding you and has never let you go. Stop trying so hard to find him and his answers and look at what's right in front of you. It's already there I promise because it's been there the whole time. He makes no mistakes and gives us just what we need. Just take a deep breath in through the nose and out through the mouth," he said as he watched her body slightly relax. "Watch God work. I've seen Him working in me just here in these moments, so I know He's working on you."

"But, you don't understand all the crap I have been through… the way I have to deal with certain things. I have to smile when I want to cry. I have to be calm when I want to scream. I have to see my situations through in my mind because if I don't and I actually live them out loud. This happens," she said as her body began to tense up and her tears streamed down like Angel Falls.

"I told you to relax, so stop it,"" he said trying to control his own emotions. Lean not to your own understanding. Just know when the time is right, all will be revealed. This is the time to reflect and stay calm. He has a plan and when you get out of your own plan He'll show you His. Stop thinking about it and it will be clear.

Start back smiling and enjoying life for its simplicities as you use to and don't worry about what you can't control. It’s that simple," he began rocking her slowly and gently his words were tranquil. "When that 'ah hah' moment hits or you get that epiphany and that gorgeous luminescent smile lights up as it will, I want to know."

Her cell phone began to ring Mel’s ringtone. "See there it is," she pushed the words out through the tears. "I just can’t deal with this. What about them? What about my friends," she turned burying her head in his chest. "How can I go back into my normal routine with all this going on?"

"I totally understand, but it’s time to guard your heart like you guard theirs," he spoke in a quiet tone. "Imagine how much they'd miss you if something were to happen to you. Stress can do some strange things. You have to come out of this angry, hurt, and disorienting place to get to the next level, and you are and have worked hard all your life. Start choosing you instead of them, then you will warrant different outcomes for you and all involved, especially your friends," he slowly rocked her and them to sleep.

Syd awaken to breakfast in bed, but no G. *Where is he*? She thought as she sat up and crawled over to the serving tray. She saw a note that read: “Hey, your clothes are in the closet. I have a special day planned for us. See you soon.” She slowly ate as she lost herself in the thoughts of what could be happening for her today.

"Still in bed, huh?" G asked walking into the room taking her out of her fantasy and into her almost unreal, reality. "Are you going to get up and get this day started with me?"

"Yes," she said pushing her tray aside and walking into what she thought was his closet. "Where are all your clothes?" she asked looking at bare walls aside from what she had bought the previous day at the mall.

"Well, since you're technically home, then you may want a place to put your things," he said walking into the closet.

"I appreciate the gesture, but don't you think it's a bit much? I mean you've seen just a peek of my roller coaster. Are you sure you want to purchase a ticket to ride this ride?" she asked, concerned he hadn't been paying attention. "What about everything? And to be honest with you, I am totally careful, but there have been some things to transpire," she said as she started to become short of breathe and began coming to terms. "I mean I am careful," she said as she started to lose her balance. The room began to spin. "Help me," she whispered as her world went dark.

"Syd, wake up. What's going on?" G yelled. He grabbed his cell, rapidly dialing 911. "Please get someone here, now," he shouted into the phone. He lifted her, taking her downstairs closer to the door. "Syd, baby, what's going on? Talk to me. Why is this happening?" The ambulance arrived. He threw the door open to let them in. "I don't know what's going on with her. One moment she was talking, the next, she was fading away and now this! What's wrong with her?" he begged for an answer.

"Sir, calm down," the male EMT asked him. "Let us figure out what's going on. Just stay calm." He went over and examined her, taking her blood pressure and vitals. He shortly returned. "She's had a seizure. These are common for her; thank goodness she has her a medical alert ring on. She will be fine, just needs a little rest, and she'll be okay."

"And the baby? The baby is fine," G asked wanting to be sure his new found family was still intact.

"Yes, the seizure didn't affect the child. Would you like my help getting her to bed?" the EMT offered.

"No, thank you," he said watching her chest rise and fall. "Why hasn't she awakened if it's just a seizure?" G thought. "Your services are no longer needed," he said aloud as he walked them to the door. He went back to her, sat her limp body up, and in a calm tender tone said, "Baby girl, please wake up. I'm afraid for you." His voice began to crack. "They say you're okay, but I don't feel that way. Please," he pleaded as his tears dawdled down his face. "Please," he whispered "I'm not going anywhere, just please."

"What's wrong, babe?" she whispered trying to remember the instants before. "What happened? Did I have a seizure? I'm sorry babe. When I get too stressed it just seems to happen. Are you okay?" she asked looking into his eyes seeing the confused hurt man inside.

"Yes, just promise to never leave, okay?" he replied, standing them up.

"I promise," she said smiling, wiping his tear stained face.

"You were trying to tell me something that you couldn't seem to put into words," he said, grabbing her hands now staring into her eyes all the way to her heart.

"I don't know," she said trying to remember exactly what she was saying as her eyes began to shift searching the room for the answers.

"Just calm down. We still have half of the day to finish and we have yet to even scratch the surface of getting ready," he said changing the subject, pointing down to his pajama bottoms.

She said, "Okay," and ran up the stairs. "I'll race ya," she said as she got halfway.

"Oh, you know what they say... cheaters never win," he said taking the steps two at a time as he caught up to her.

She belted out a huge childlike laugh. "Well, you're cheating. You have a home court advantage," she said as she still raced down the hall.

"No, I don't seeing as we both will soon live here," he said turning into the bedroom and plopping on the bed.

She slowed her pace at the door and that's when it hit her, "HOME," she said aloud. "That's what it was, babe," she said out of breathe.

He sat up, looking at her. "That, baby is working on you. We need to go to baby yoga or something," he chuckled.

She looked at him seriously with a blank stare. "I don't know who my child's father is," she said in a bland far away voice and began to turn to walk back out of what she thought would be his life.

"Oh, you don't get to leave me like that. We are in this thing together, you and me, so we will figure it out. You still keep that calendar?"

"Yea, why?" she asked with a puzzled look on her face.

"Do you want to know or are you okay with how things are," he asked hoping he hadn't overstepped.

"No, I'm fine," she lied remembering its synced in her phone. "My possibilities are not the best choices for me, and there are only three, just so you know." She didn't want to turn around and face him.

He walked up behind her, put one arm around her shoulders, and the other around her waist. "I love you. Do you want to lay in bed with the smell of cold maple syrup in the air until you feel like moving around again?" he kissed her cheek.

"Yes," she shook her head again. There is a man that can love a woman through all of this? Wow, he's simply amazing.

"Okay, you want to spoon me or I spoon you? Or you want to sleep feet to head, or you want to lie on my chest, or you want me to lay on yours?" he said in an innocent tone, jokingly.

"I choose…. D, all of the above," she said with an uncontrollable grin. Her eyes lit up and sparkled as she turned to look at him. "Thank you for always saying the right things." She kissed him. "You are truly the best," she said.

"Well, let's get this lazy day started. You, me, and us being," he said bouncing down onto the bed. She bounced down and felt all the breakfast wanting to come up. "No, no, no," he said as he grabbed the dinner tray to catch what was originally on the tray, but that was only the beginning. She hurled that little up and high-tailed it into the bathroom where she hugged his lavatory for what seemed like dear life. The way her back arched, and her body jerked and jolted as it released from her body, made him cringe because he was helpless. As she finished, he rubbed her back, gave her a washcloth for her face, and ran her a quick bath where she added a hint of baby oil, to keep the future stretchmark away. She got in and soaked to relieve some of the tension brought on by the vomiting and the stress from her unknown sadness. She laid there drifting in and out of sleep. "Babe, did you forget about our cuddling?" G reminded her softly.

"Oh no, this water just feels so good, ya know?" she said standing for the towel she thought was on the stand just beside the tub, but it was farther than she expected, and she slipped. G tried to catch her as she hit her side on the side of the pedestal. A loud thump shook G's soul.

"Are you okay," he said scooping her into his arms?

"Yeah, just hurts a little," she said rubbing her side. "Guess today just isn't my day, huh?" she giggled.

"Are we going to the ER now?" he said with no giggle or any sense of play in his voice.

"No, silly it's was a minor fall. I am fine." She wiggled out of his arms, grabbing the towel. "We are going to cuddle remember?"

"Cuddle? That baby better be okay, Syd. You, ugh, I don't know," he said walking out of the bathroom noticeably frazzled.

"Babe, I'm okay," she said following him. There was baby oil in the tub. It was a little slick and I slipped. That's all. We," she said pointing to her belly, "are okay."

"Okay, just be okay. Okay?" he said walking over to her, kissing her forehead.

"I promise. Now, can I have that shirt you had on? I love your scent."

He smiled. "How about I give you this one?" he said pulling his shirt over his head.

"Great," she said as he slipped it over her head. "Ooooh, and it's already warm." She walked over to the bed looking behind her to make sure he was coming, too.

"Oh, don't worry, I'm never too far from you," he said as he lay on the bed and positioned himself so she could lie on his chest as they both fell asleep.

"Babe, wake up. We're going to be late," G said jumping out the bed looking at the time.

"What time is it?" she asked looking around trying to wake completely up.

"It's 6:30. Babe, please get up and get dressed. We are going to be late," he begged calmly.

"Okay, I'm up," she said gathering her thoughts and sitting up. "Honey, would you get my clothes out the closet, please?" She scratched her head realizing her hair was a total mess. "Oh my goodness, we may be late!" She sprang off the bed and ran in to the restroom. "So, if you held me the entire time I slept, who cleaned in here?" she said looking around.

"I have housekeepers, honey. They come in and tidy things up, like the breakfast you ate and replaced on the tray. Why do you ask?" he yelled from his closet.

"I was just wondering," she said looking for anything to fix her hair with.

"So how are you coming in there?" he asked her just as he was walking in.

"I'm making it," she said finally finding a cabinet with more than enough hair care supplies for both of them. Suddenly, she heard the soft sounds of Jamie Foxx came through the bathroom and bedroom. "Fifteen Minutes." She smiled. "Babe, no, you said we were running late."

"All I need is fifteen minutes, I promise. Maybe not even that if you cooperate," he said sneaking up behind her, nibbling her neck. "Hey, come here .Let me tell you what happened last night," he said leading her back to the bedroom.

"Last night. Huh?" She said remembering she always enjoyed what he had to "say" about last night.

"Yep," he said laying her on the bed, placing deep passionate kisses on her like they had just reunited for the first time. "Queen you came back to me," he whispered through kisses. Kneeling over her, he sat up just to admire what a woman he had before him. She smiled at him. *I love this* he thought as he leaned in down and their lips slowly met. As they touched, he felt her sweet breathe on his lips, and it made him rock hard. She flicked her tongue to tease his lips. He pressed their lips together as his tongue slowly entered her lips.

She moaned, "Babe." He kissed her cheek, slipping down to her neck. She giggled seductively, only making him want to pleasure her more. He pulled her T-shirt over her head and slowly kissed down her chest down to her baby bump. He kissed and rubbed there as he caressed her spot to warm it before he got there. He squirmed in anticipation. He kissed right below her belly, still fingering the inside with his pointer finger, and gently massaging her clit with his thumb. "Babe wait, wait, wait," she begged. He knew it was time he began to softly and gently kiss her clit and slowly picked up the pace as her body told him exactly what to do. He sucked gently, then more aggressively, to release her clit with a slight nibble. As her body tensed, he sucked as if it were his last bit of oxygen. And he needed every last drop. She moaned as her body tapped out.

"See, babe, it was less than fifteen minutes, I only needed a taste," he smiled as he sat beside her on the bed. He rubbed her hair. "You are so beautiful," he said losing himself in her eyes.

She smiled, grabbed his arm, and said, "Now, we're going to be late. I want more, or at least a cuddle."

He smiled, wrapped her in his arms. "No more. Here is your cuddle. Come on, babe. We have to go," he smiled at her, shaking his head.

"Ugh, babe," she whined, "but I want more," holding his arms as they were wrapped around her.

"Later, I promise. Whatever you like, queen, but right now we have to eat, among other things," he sat them up, "so go get ready, and so will I okay, deal?"

"Deal," she agreed, "but I want a kiss first," she said already puckered up.

"I seal this deal with a kiss," he said leaning in for a kiss.

She grabbed his neck and wrapped her legs around his waist. "Ha I got ya now," she said as she placed small pecks on his lips, ending with her parting his lips, her tongue entering his mouth searching for his tongue. "I love you, Greg, and thank you for saving me and being so much more."

"No problem, queen, just returning the favor," he said repositioning. "Now, are you going to get ready or is my stomach going to continue to touch my back?" he asked rubbing his empty belly

"Oh, we have to feed the baby," she said mocking him as she got up and half skipped to the shower. "Out in two shakes. My hair will be ready so two birds okay," she said not expecting a response.

"Okay, honey," he said brushing his teeth, then hair, then washed his face and out the bathroom he went. He grabbed his clothes and shoes and threw them on. "Babe, I'm ready, and I'm going to get the car," he yelled into the bathroom and off he went.

Syd was out of the shower, hair pulled up, and brushing her teeth. She hurried through her processes. She walked in the bedroom, grabbed her dress, slid it over her head, slipped her shoes on, out the bedroom and down the hall she walked again admiring his home. *This house is amazing. Three-story with ten bedrooms that came straight from a magazine, seven full and three half bathrooms, which are all immaculately dressed, an office on the first and second floors, a marble kitchen with a nook, an island and stainless steel everything, the entrance room has a six-foot chandelier, an indoor/outdoor pool off the side of the house, with a basketball court and a recreational area. I love this house*! She thought as she walked down the left staircase.

"Babe you need any help, or are you okay? I was coming to help. How's your side? I saw it had gotten a little dark and bruised," he asked as he hurried to her side.

"I'm fine. Let's get to this date," she smiled. "Where are we going?" she asked as she watched the last few steps?

"Well, we can go to The Majestic Grille. I know how you love that place, or..." he began saying.

"Sold, I want to go there; they have my favorite smoked salmon EVER," she said as her mouth began to water.

"Okay, great. There is a roof top deal going on downtown, and I wanted to go. Are you up for it? He asked helping her into his Porsche.

"Yeah, am I dressed for it?" she asked really wondering about if being pregnant was appropriate for the function.

"Babe, you are TOTALLY fine," he said catching her sentiments and putting her at ease.

"Oh, okay," she said as he pulled out his drive.

They got a spot close to the door at The Majestic Grille. They ordered, ate, and dinner went smoothly. All her food stayed down. Things were going well until she looked up and there was a drunken Colby with some white lady holding him up. Syd's face had panic all over it as he landed right at her table.

"This seat taken?" Colby said as he plopped down at their table.

"I am so sorry," the lady said to Colby, "honey, please let's go. You're embarrassing us."

"Nope, you remember about six or seven months ago? Wait, how many months are you?" he slurred at Syd. "Don't matter. That's yo step child," he pointed to Syd's belly.

"Excuse, me, sir, that alcohol must be pretty strong, but my fiancée and I conceived that child on the south of France and only recently reentered the states," G said looking at Colby as if he had a third eye. As the waiter passed, G asked for the check.

"So you think, “Colby leaned in, "she don’t drink, so it’s easy to take advantage of a person like that," he winked as his foul alcohol assaulted G as Colby’s words insulted Syd.

"What are you saying, Colby?" the lady asked.

"Look, shut up, Bethany. You ain’t got shit on her and I will leave yo ass if you don’t get it together," Colby threatened.

"You need a good, lawyer?" Syd gave her a card to one up him.

G paid the check, as he helped Syd out of her seat. "Stay away from my fiancée or there will be more pressing matters at hand," G looked Colby directly in his eyes just before walking Syd to the car.

"Go get the car. She’s in real estate, she’s not a real lawyer," Colby said to Bethany slapping her on the ass.

"You know this card seems legit. I’ll go get the car," she said as she walked out of the door trying to catch Syd before they pulled off. "Ma’am, ma’am, I know my husband and I know your fiancée says south of France, but this is not the first time, and if you are a lawyer I could really use your help," she said holding back tears. "He’s a monster, and we have children. He will take them and everything, please."

"Just call the office Monday. Tell Toni you have my card. Explain everything; she will have you set up. You have nothing to worry about, please .If he is as bad as you say, get out now. People like that don't get better; they get far worse," Syd said empathizing with her going into lawyer mode.

"Thank you, and if what he's saying is true, my deepest apologies. He only sees happiness for himself," she said as she ran to the car, started it, and drove away.

G, grabbed Syd's hand before she began to explain and asked, "Still up for some rooftop mingling?"

She just looked at him, trying to control the tears. "Wow," she breathed out and shook her head. "Yes," wanting to walk through his mind to see exactly what he wanted so she could mold herself and become just that.

He played calm sultry music on the ride. As they entered the downtown traffic, he looked at her and said, "Are you ready to turn up?"

"Yes, I sure am," she said actually ready to dance and let loose.

He changed the mood in the car and played Yo Gotti and a K. Michelle mix because they are only Memphis' finest.

He parked in a garage. They walked over to the party and went to the top floor. When the elevator door opened, they partied as if they were teenagers. She twerked for him. He grinded on her. They laughed, met some new people, and took more than a few pictures. He drank a little more than he wanted to. The night flew by. 3:00 a.m. came and they were heading to the car laughing and reminiscing about moments just passed. "Babe, I can't drive all the way back home. You want to stay down here?" he asked.

"Okay," she said as a yawn escaped her lips.

"Oh, you're tired, too, huh? Well, here we come Peabody. Hopefully, the ducks are put away. I can't afford one of those jokers," he said jokingly.

"Yeah," she said laying her head back, drifting in and out of sleep.

He drove them around the corner and into the parking garage of the Peabody Hotel and got their room. She took the quickest shower she'd ever taken in life, and he followed. As soon as their heads hit the pillows, they were fast asleep.

G got up, called the desk asking about a place to get a suit and shoes. He spoke softly not wanting to wake Syd.

"Babe, you're leaving me here?" Syd asked in a confused tone.

"No, well, yes, but it's just a quick meeting, and its downtown like a block from here. I will be right back. I meant to be back before you awakened."

Theirs was a tap on the door. "Room service," a quiet voice said, G tiptoed over to the door with his wallet in hand. He was handed a very small bag, a standing dress bag, box of shoes, and a suit that looked tailor made for him. He placed the small bag in the nightstand, slipped his suit on, looked over at Syd, and said, "Babe, I apologize. I will make it quick," he said trying to avoid eye contact due to his weakness for her.

"Baby, do you have to leave?" she asked seductively. "Well, at least can I have a kiss, you know, for the wait?"

He turned, chuckling and shaking his head. "Of course, queen. You know I can never say no to you ever." Walking towards the bed in the overpriced room in the Peabody Place Hotel, he gently kissed her lips, caressed her face, while looking deeply into her eyes, and said, "Okay, that's enough for now, I have a meeting to get to."

She grabbed the collar of his shirt while kissing him deeply, sliding her hand down his torso, only stopping at his belt, unbuckling it.

"Whoa, now, queen are you sure you're ready for this? You don't have to. I love you enough to play by your rules and to take my time," he assures her.

"Baby, I want this and you more than anything I have ever wanted. You have truly made my life this past week. You are everything, patient, kind, and a total embodiment of what love is and should be." She pulled him closer, then pushed his upper body up to become face-to-face with his already rock hard manhood. She began kissing and slightly nibbling the tip through his pant, while unzipping them and setting it free. She licked up the side as if it were her favorite chocolate ice cream, approaching the tip. She sucked until it exited her lips with a slight pop, which made his entire body shiver. She took him entirely into her mouth and began to deep throat him until her mouth was dripping and she could hear him moaning out loud. He sat on the bed as she went into the bathroom to rinse his fluids out and brush her teeth; she came back in and sat on the side of the bed as he stood watching her, smiling.

"Queen you are the best. I want you to be my wife and lifetime partner," he began.

"Baby you can have all of me, everything I own," she said interrupting him.

Stopping her, he kneeled as they became eye-to-eye. "I want you, every piece and part of you. Don't just let it end with this week; I want this to be the start of us until eternity. I know the feelings you have for Damion, but I NEED you, all of you. I can't wait any longer. This is our chance, our opportunity. Please say yes, please say yes." He reached into the nightstand and grabbed a little black box, opened it, to reveal a four carat, princess cut, rose-gold, platinum trimmed engagement ring and repeated, "Please, say YES!"

"Yes, yes, yes, a million times yes," she whispered in amazement. "You can't be real! What did I do to deserve such a man?" she said aloud, looking at him astonished. "Wow babe, you are truly my king! I love you G, and thank you for being who you are! I love, love, love, you!!!"

He stood them both up with one scoop of their bodies. "I have wanted you since day one." He began to undress her already almost fully naked body. A soft caress of her shoulder to slide the right strap off her shoulder, then a gentle stroke on the left led the other strap off her shoulder and guided the entire dress to the floor. He took a step back to admire her unclothed body, and then kneeled to her belly and said, "I promise to be here for you forever and a day." Kissing her tummy oh so softly, he raised his body. "Are you ready?" he asked taking her into his arm.

She simply nodded, "Yes."

He placed her body down onto the king sized bed and began to lay sweet subtle kisses on her lips, dabbing his tongue in and out of her mouth, making her thirst for more. Moving down to her neck kissing and sucking all the while tracing from one place to the next, making her moan silently and biting her tongue; continuing down to her breasts, left then right adoring each nipple with a meticulous rhythm filled with kisses, sucks, and small nibbles. "Oh my," he murmured almost there momentarily looking up with a smile. He slowly examined her masterpiece as if he's couldn't determine where to start. He flicked his tongue on her clit, then moved down to the vulva kissing it ever so delicately. "Hello, beautiful." We meet again," he said to the lips he didn't want to leave only hours earlier, while leisurely sliding two fingers inside. He came up briefly to examine the excited and anxious face she couldn't hide as her eyes begin to glisten, where he planted the most sensual kisses on her lips, which caused her to erupt all over his hand. "Wow, queen, didn't know you could do that. Let's see what my tongue will do between your other lips."

Again, speechless, she bit her lip and shook her head.

He kissed her clit then, sucked it until it swelled in his mouth as she squirted all over his chin. "Oh, baby, I love the way you taste," he exclaimed as he continued to make her squirt repeatedly by flicking his tongue and finger simultaneously.

She screamed out in pleasure, "Damn babe, I'm ready for you come and give it to me. Pleeeeeaaaaaassssssseeeee, Daddy give me you all of you," she said pulling him up so his rock hard, dark chocolate, just her size dick could enter her waiting vagina.

He slowly entered with a loud, but timid, moan. "Ooooooohhhhhhh, you gone make me nut, just feeling the lips on my little head."

She giggled "I know you better than that, and you can hold out give it to me!"

Nice and slow, he grabbed the remote and Usher's "Nice and Slow" began to play." I got you my lady, just remember to enjoy." He wraps her legs around him and he stood them against the wall, while deeply kissing her. He plows into her ever so slowly one hand on her ass supporting her, the other holding her hand sensually.

She feels every vein in his penis as it goes in and out, squirting all over the wall, floor and him. She whimpered in pleasure. "I can't stop the tears. Oh, my goodness you are amazing, baby. I can't wait to be your wife. Make love to me; make love to me please…" she said begging.

He gently laid her on the bed, he sped up the love, while holding her hips, and he thrust himself inside soft, but hard at the same time. "Let me take you to the moon and back." Right as he was about to cum, he laid his chest onto her breasts looking directly into her eyes, grabbing both her hands. "I love you," he said in a heavy deep breath and he exploded inside her.

Friendship

"Hey, lady," I answered the phone.

"What are you up to? Mel asked.

"Oh, nothing. Creating a check list for tomorrow and scheduling me a spa day for later today, I want a massage, mani, and pedi. You joining me, right?" Syd asked hopeful

"Yeah, yeah, if I hadn't called you wouldn't have said anything and would have gone alone. But, it's cool. I know that baby got you scatter brain over there," she said in a blasé tone. "Have you talked to Damion yet? I don't mean to pry, but I thought we were better than this. Does our friendship not mean anything to either of you? I am tired of being in the middle."

"Honey," Syd said stretching across her bed, "he made a choice and until I can live with it and be okay dealing with all of it, I have to be away from him. You know the way I felt about him. You know this baby will one day want to know who its father is and what will I be able to say? If it is him: Well, that's him over there with his family; you can look, but don't get to close. Um, no thank you I'll spare us all that drama and do the necessary and deal with separating myself from him right now. You were raised in a single parent household. Turned out great and your mom was barely making ends meet."

"Ugh, Syd, you are so damn stubborn," she said slightly annoyed. "Please talk to him. PLEASE?"

"Girl, boo!" Syd said in her not in a million years voice. "He doesn't deserve me; anyway, the place is in Collierville. The Gould's Spa out there, appointment time is in two hours. Please be on time, and not colored people time!"

"I will, so how is my little niece or nephew? When do we get to go and look at the baby?" she asked enthusiastically. "I want to see if it looks like you or D, G, or Colby."

"See that foolishness, there! If I could slap you through the phone that cheek would be red!" Syd said in her "stop playing" voice. "Who is ringing my door bell? Girl if it's one of these Jehovah's Witnesses I am going to start speaking in tongues!"

"Girl, you so crazy," she said. "Are you going to get up? Don't sound like you moving around at all?"

"Ugh, I just want to rest for a little while. Maybe they'll go away," Syd said kicking her feet tantrum style. "Ugh, there it is again."

"Get up!" Mel said yelling.

"Ugh, if it's you at this door and you have a key I swear fo cheese and crackers, we gone fight," Syd said aggravated as hell having to get out of her warm bed.

"Chile open the door, and it ain't me. Let me get myself together to get to this spa day! Bye, chic," she said giggling.

Syd hung up and slowly walked to the front door dreading every step. "I wondered who could be at my door, and why Jesus, why?"

"Open the door, please Chryssany," a deep, but familiar voice rang out through the door.

"I am coming," she barely shouted. Getting closer to the door, she recognized the silhouette. Instantly, her heart began to race. "Again, why Jesus?" she said trying to calm down before she open the door and contain all her mixed emotions.

"Open the door Syd. I can see you. We need to talk and you can't avoid me anymore. I won't let you," he said.

"Is this a set up?" she thought. Did he and Mel plan this? "Ugh," shaking her head. "I don't believe this. Here I come, Damion," she said reaching for the handle.

"Yeah, that's it now, turn the lock and let me in," he instructed again through the door.

"What's up?" she said opening the door and letting him in. "What can I do for you?"

"You can talk to me, and acknowledge our million year old friendship and the pact we made to never stay mad at each other and to always talk it out," he said with a pitiful look and a crack of sadness in his voice.

"While I hear you and vaguely remember said pact, seems as if that's something a husband and wife would agree to, not just mere friends, ya know?" she stated bluntly moving slightly to the side to allow him access to her home.

Stepping in, he said, "Wow pregnancy looks good on you. Why are you being this way, why won't you talk to me and let us come to a resolve? You love me right?"

"Umm, yea that's debatable," she said holding back a laugh. "I always thought you and I were the epitome of love, but we were not. We, however, were just a couple of friends who knew how to get our rocks off, the perfect people to go to get what we wanted and how we wanted, without any attachments."

"Wow, didn't know you thought of us like that. Maybe I should leave," he said motioning for the door.

"Maybe so," she said re-opening the front door. "If you want to leave, please by all means."

"Talk to me," Damion pleaded.

"Talk to you about what?" she questioned. "There is really no conversation to be had. You made a well-informed, knowledgeable decision about me or us, and didn't consult me. So there is absolutely no conversation to be had on that subject."

"Well, Chryssany, since you want to be like that, you did the same about the child growing inside you," he said with questioning eyes.

"Excuse you? How dare you bring my child into this drama? I never said this was your child," she said rubbing her little bulge. "Even if it were, you have clearly shown me your priority list, and I am not on it. Hell, your loyalty is to her so why are you even here? I'm always on the outside looking in so, I took time away to clear my mind and heart."

"Yeah, you took a week from Mel, but me, you need almost a month; that small conference call doesn't matter. You left me high and dry." He stepped in closer

"Why would I want to know a man who puts me second, tells me lies just to manipulate a moment of pleasure out of me, and then marries a woman just because 'he's a man'? Why would I allow myself to be used by a man I held in such high regards, only to find out he is far worse than any of the ones I ever could've imagined! So high and dry is the nice way out in my opinion," she said feeling tragically hurt, sad, and totally misunderstood.

"Can we please sit and talk like adults? Please Syd," he said begging as he pulled her toward the great room.

"Why do we NEED to sit or even talk?" she said dramatically snatching her arm away from him.

"Because, obviously, there are some unresolved issues here that you I and need to clear up," he said holding out his hand.

"I will talk with you," she said walking passed him, towards the large comfy sectional style crimson and silver, couch.

"Great," he said plopping down on the couch. First, why throw me away? You know the way I feel about you and us. Why give up on a beautiful friendship like ours?"

Syd said rolling her eyes, "Because it really isn't worth it and you actually threw me away first. In all honesty, I knew there would be trials and I knew some things would get in the way, but I always thought I would be your misses, not just a guest at your wedding. All those years of promises and…"

"I know, Syd," he said interrupting her. "But, I implore you to see this from my perspective. She is pregnant, my first born. I can't just walk away from that. I have to do what a man is supposed to do."

"You aren't even sure if that is your child, while on the other hand I can guarantee you, ugh, you know what? It isn't worth it," she said catching his gaze.

"What can you guarantee, Chryssany, tell me!" he said looking her square in the eyes. "I need to be 100%

sure about everything before I can make an educated decision about my future; which leads me to my second point. When are you going to bring up the father of your child when do we get to know your big secret?"

"I can guarantee you that, I and my child are and will be taken great care of," she said moving to the love seat, looking around for the remote. "Why is it such a big deal who my 'baby daddy' is?"

"Chryssany, I have always, just wanted you," he said with a soft look on his face and an apologetic tone. "Please don't shut me out like you always do. I have loved you since the eighth grade, girl. I will fight for you and have been for the past 12 years. Syd, please I beg you," he went down on one knee. "If you have any type of care, love, I will even take pity, for me don't shut me out. I need you. You have been a part of my make up for as long as I can remember." Tears began to flow down his face and his voice began to crack. "Baby girl, I have always been yours, you have and will always be my best friend. No one can ever take the place of you. You taught me how to love, how to deal with rejection, and how a true relationship works. Not by manipulation, but by undeniable trust and love. Please, baby girl, please."

She leaned in close to his face, put her hand on his cheeks, as he placed his hand on top of hers. "We will always be friends. I just need to get passed these hurt feelings." She picked up my remote to play her song on surround sound. "You want to know how hurt I have been? And add in the pregnancy hormones.... You know I suck with verbal communication," so she hit play; and sounds of Jill Scott rang out her love:

{Intro}: Yo, I'm tripping right,

I heard you got married.

You got married?

No I mean, make any sense

I mean, it's not like I, I didn't think you were seeing other people or whatever,

I mean I was seeing other people but

You know what this is,

You know what it was, you tsch

I can't say I really understand though

Damion grabbed the remote and turned the volume down almost completely. "I feel that, but when you chose Alex in the ninth grade I had to deal with it, you remember that Rome CD, only one song; '*Every Time*' I belong to you? I knew back then no one could care for you like I do. Syd, you belong to me and only me. Even back then I told you if I married someone else, you would still hold my heart. Throughout high school, you took Alex and forgot me. That shit hurt dreadfully, but you still talked to me every night. When life was hard, you ran to me. When nothing made sense, you ran to me."

"You were my rock and have been, but now I'm in the cold," she said through short breaths and tears. "I truly needed you during this ordeal, and you are being someone who doesn't deserve me. Damn, I know I have messed up in the past, but you were never supposed to move on. You were supposed to be mine. The tears won't stop, I can't be around you, knowing I'm not the end for you and you're not it for me. I wanted to give my whole self to you, I wanted to be everything for you, but you chose her over and over again. How do you expect me to react when you love me for a minute and the love goes away? I want a lifetime love, not a momentary mishaps like... ugh just not this. Stay away from me, please! As adults we are too old to keep playing this back and forth game," she said removing him from the life she thought they would have by then. "She took my spot in all my future plans, your heart, and in both of our realities."

Damion wrapped his arms around her. "I will always be your Damion; ALWAYS, no matter what."

"You can't be serious," she said removing myself from his tender cuddle. "How can that be possible?" she said backing away from him putting some space in between the man she had always thought was her future, the man she thought was her forever knight and shining armor. "I can't keep playing this game; every time I let my guard down; you sneak in and attack my heart. This isn't high school and soon children will be involved," she said walking towards her bedroom. "I will not allow my son or daughter to see me be manipulated by a person I have been in love with since day one."

"What are you saying, Chryssany? I can't be your friend if I marry someone else?" he said following her down my corridor and into the bedroom. "Why do you always run from me or push me away? I am your day one, and I have always reciprocated that love. You know that! Chryssany stop, just stop running from me and talk to me. I can't lose you, Please see this from my point of view."

Reaching the bedroom, she plopped down onto the teal bedspread. "If you loved me, you wouldn't ask that of me. I wish I could tell you everything, but I am so afraid of your reaction."

"Tell me. We may never get this chance again," he said kneeling in front of her, rubbing her baby filled belly with the most sincerity in his eyes that she'd seen in a long time.

"I honestly wish I could, but some things have their moment and sometimes we miss those moments," she said staring into his eyes, placing her hand on top of his. "And, this moment has surely passed. I won't keep pretending that this will get better or change, but I will stay in the reality where you are no longer mine."

"I have an affair with you in my mind every time we speak. When you cross my mind, when any one mentions your name, I smell your perfume. You are all I think of," he said repositioning his body to stand before her. "You have been all I wanted since we met." He began wiping her tears away. "You have encompassed every thought since we were in high school," he said, kissing her through each word. "Chryssany, you still give me butterflies." He was lifting her T-shirt over her head.

"Stop, please, D, we can't," she said trying to resist the man she thought to be her everything, the one man she couldn't say no to, the man that she couldn't see past.

"If you truly want me to stop, I will, but don't say no when you really mean yes." He began to undress slowly, his V-neck polo shirt, over his head exposing that chest and those abs, chiseled, almost God like. Her mouth began to water. "Syd, say something."

She had no words, only lifted her bottom to assist him in the removal of her panties.

"So you'll be mine forever and a day right?" he said sliding out of his freshly pressed Polo shorts and loafers.

She nodded agreeing with every inch of her soul.

He slowly and gently lifted her body while arranging himself comfortably so he could slide right in. He began slowly, looking her in the eyes. "Baby, we are stuck together. No one can break what we have. I promise you have been, and will always be, my top priority," he said making her doubts melt and soak the bed with all her passion. He moved as if they were becoming one, kissing where her tears had fallen, wrapping her in his love. He ran his fingers through her freshly pressed hair. "I love you, Chryssany," he said as he thrust still slow, grabbing her right leg, holding it up to penetrate what seemed like her heart. "It feels so right," he whispered. "Babe, let me do you how you like." She smiled. He removed his shiny, thick, long penis just enough to allow her to turn over on her stomach. "Open up," he said. She did as instructed; he entered me with a moan. "Damn, it's so good." He lifted his leg so she could cross hers. As he pushed in, she held her position then as he drew back, she tightened and inhaled so he could feel her wanting ALL of him. His body shivered as she tightened around him. "Oh baby, I won't last like this." He grabbed the top of the mattress to stabilize his position. As he went deeper, she moaned, "Ooohhhhhh please don't leave me with tears running down my face." He lowered himself where his chest tenderly touched her back.

He leaned in. "I am all yours forever. Never forget that, baby girl." With that she felt he emptied himself inside of her soul.

They both got up. He ran her a bath just the way she liked it. He led her into the master bathroom where her old school footed bath tub awaited her arrival, with the water just at the top, no bubbles only the bath fizzes handmade by Little Bird. He helped her in and watched her lower herself into the bath. He then pulled her hair into a bun and with the rubber band he always wore on his wrist and secured it. Next, he placed himself right behind her in the bath. The water overflowed and splashed all over the bathroom floor. She laughed. "Look at you, making another mess."

"Another?" he said.

"Yep, those sheets though," she laughed again.

"Are we good? I need you Chryssany; we're stuck together like you always said back in the day," he said lathering up the bath sponge.

"Yes, just don't make me feel less than adequate. Are you seriously going to marry this broad?" she asked leaning forward as he ran the soap filled water down her neck onto her back.

"I don't know, Syd. My dad passed away at an early age, and I felt alone with just my mom. She didn't understand most of what I was going through and was barely making it. I never want that for my son. If in fact, this is my child."

Syd turned around to wash his chest and asked, "What do you mean IF? You two were having unprotected sex, right? You did release into her right?" she questioned more aggressively than she should have.

"If I didn't know any better I would swear you were pushing me towards the marriage," he said removing the sponge from her hand.

"What? No, it's just that facts are facts, ya know? And don't say if and you participated, too," she said trying to clean up her anger.

"Yeah, I will own up to my doings, but we use protection. Yes the condom broke a couple times, but I don't remember our dates lining up with this pregnancy," he said actually thinking about the dates. "In all honesty I have a better, much more accurate shot of being your child's father. Now, that makes sense," he said coming out of the clouds and landing smack dab in her face.

She jumped up, attempting to rush out of the bath, almost slipping right down into the tub.

"Syd, slow down," he said in a sturdy but caring tone.

"You know I can't sit in the water too long," she said still scurrying to get out the bath.

"Yeah, but let me help you, I want to be sure the baby doesn't get hurt with your clumsy tail," he said raising out of the bath while letting the water out then grabbing the towel off the holder. "Here, baby girl." He put the towel on her shoulders heading to the linen closet for his own towel.

"Thanks," she said slowing down, remembering her little bun. She smiled as she dried her body and walked back into the bedroom.

He said following her with his towel wrapped around his waist, "Which drawer is mine?"

She giggled. "You ain't got no drawer here."

"Quit playing. Which one?" he said not looking back as her examined my dresser.

"The middle one," she whispered.

"Say no more. I'm glad you spoke up. I would hate to walk out of here in yo draws," he said pulling out a pair of fresh boxers.

She draped herself across the bed, not attempting to do anything but rest. While he dressed, he asked, "So what's the big deal with you and who your child's dad is and the sex of the baby? What's the big secret?" he asked.

"No secret, just keeping my business to myself. The less people know, the less they worry about," she said in a nonchalant tone

"Well, just so you know," he said walking towards her, "I will always be yours lady," kissing her forehead. "I will continue from now to the end of time to prove that to you. You will always be my best friend, no matter who my wife is, I pinky promise. "His cell began to ring "Don't listen to what people say; they don't know about you and me." "I'm sorry I have to take this," he said backing out of the bedroom.

"What's up?" he answered. A loud inaudible sound came rattling back into the bedroom.

"Must be the ole ball and chain there," she said sucking her teeth, hopping off the bed.

"You're what?" he exclaimed. "I'm on my way! I got to go baby girl, but remember what I said best friends forever." Then he dashed out the front door.

He dashed through traffic

"What do you mean we're in labor? We are only six months? What's developed? Is the baby safe, are you sure your water broke?" Damion asked panicking.

"Yeah, just get me to the damn hospital; I'm in a lot of pain!" Mika said in an irritated and annoyed voice.

"Okay, I got the bag and the car seat. Do you want me to carry you down the steps or you got it?" Damion asked.

"I can get down the damn steps by myself, Papi; just get me out of here!!!" she sang out in pain.

Damion's cell phone rang. "Hello, I can't talk now, I'm having a baby," he yelled in the phone.

"I know. Syd told me. What hospital? We'll meet you guys there," Mel asked in a hurried tone as she was getting ready to walk out the door.

"Babe, the Women's Hospital, right?" Damion yelled to the car as he locked the door?

"Yes, Papi, but whhhhyyyyyy oh em gee get this thing out of me!!!" Again, Shamika said singing out in pain.

"Okay, got it. We'll see you there," Mel said.

"Yep, I'm on my way, too," Syd said chiming in on the three-way.

"Aight," Damion said in an exasperated tone.

"So it's safe to say, I need to cancel our spa treatments?" Syd asked in a very serious melodramatic tone.

"You are so silly. Stop playing. You know you want to support him. I know the circumstances surrounding this, but I also know you; and selfish and/or petty are both unlikely characteristics," Mel said cruising down Interstate 240. "Have you left the house yet?"

"Yes and no. I was trying to make sure I would be comfortable and not be too cold, and then I thought it might to hot. So, I went in to find something else to put on, but I felt that little jogging suit you bought me last year would be perfect, so I wore that," she said, explaining why she hadn't left the house yet.

"Whatever, I will turn this damn car around and get you if you don't start that damn truck up and pull the fuck of in this direction," Mel said in a motherly manner.

"Okay," Syd said. "The car was already on for your information. I just think it will be a bit odd. What if I hold it? What do I say? Hello, little person you will soon be a big brother or sister; ugh this is so freaking embarrassing!"

"No, it isn't. It is life," Mel said in a matter-of-fact demeanor, "Look I am about to get off on Walnut Grove, so I am almost there. Please put on your big girl draws and bring your ass! Suck it up, girl."

"I am getting on the expressway; I'll be there in like 15 minutes," Syd said with a sigh.

"Cool, we can talk for 15 more minutes. So what's new in your life that I don't already know about?" she asked probing. "Don't say nothing, I peeped that gorgeous rock out. SO, what's the T or do I need to call Alex? I know he knows. You always tell him first," she said in an incriminating voice.

"No, I don't. I seldom talk to him; you should know that. He is always so busy. I don't even think he knows about my pregnancy," she said trying to swiftly change the subject.

"Yes, he does, honey. I told him when you decided to take some time off," she said in a checkmate voice. "Although, it kind of slipped out because I was concerned you had gone missing and everything, I didn't know. Plus, I thought you'd already told him," she said trying to clean up that she had spilled the beans.

"God dang it, Mel. Why can't you just keep the secrets that I ask you to?" Syd said almost in tears. "It isn't the fact that you told him this it's the fact that you always feel the need to tell MY freaking business. You don't fucking listen. Damn, Mel you can't hold water. This just ain't right."

"Please calm down; you are driving. If you need to, pull over. I am sorry," she said pleading. "Where are you? I will meet you."

"I'm fine," Syd said clearing her throat and getting her thoughts together. "Just please don't share anymore of my business without my approval. Damn, Mel, can you do that for me? I am getting off on Walnut Grove now."

"Okay, I promise," she said breathing hard. "You had me scared. You are a tiny pregnant person, and I want to meet my best friend's' kid so please be careful."

"I will. Where did you park?" Syd asked searching for her.

"Right here," she said in a dry tone.

"Ugh, I promise sometimes, I wish I could kill you and get away with it," Syd said in an irritated voice. "I am over here by the door where the pregnant people go in."

"Duh, look to your left," she said waving her left hand over her head.

"Oh, hey chic," Syd said in a slightly embarrassed tone.

"Yep, saved you a spot, right next to me," she said standing in a vacant spot.

"Okay, move," Syd said leaning on her horn "and hang up. The feedback from the echo is going to make me throw up."

"Okay, let's do this. She's in labor of course. She started pushing about 10 minutes ago. Hadn't gotten a text update since. Room number 332. Baby is under her last name because they aren't married," Mel said giving all the updates.

"Well, aren't you in the know?" Syd said nudging her in the arm.

"Of course, I am going to be an aunt." Syd looked at her and wanted to spit fire, but tried to shake it off.

"Sorry, boo. This is his kid, too, so you have to be open to being an aunt," she said explaining as they got on the elevator.

"Look, first of all stop all this, too, also, and all that. This is my baby in my belly, and until I am ready to share his/her father with the world, it's mine and mine alone! You got that chic?" she said cornering her with her little protruding belly between Mel and the elevator doors.

"You have become hostile with this pregnancy; I hope your baby ain't mean, too. I hear you, and I will keep all those comments to myself," she said almost falling out of the elevator doors.

"Wow, she had a quick labor. They are in recovery. The baby is healthy and he's a bit concerned," she said not looking up from reading the text messages as they came in.

"Okay, where can we sit down? Do we need to go to the gift shop and pick something up?" Syd asked, wondering if it was impolite to come in empty handed.

"Damn, how much stuff do we have to buy? I bought for the baby shower I wasn't invited to. She got a whole damn travel system from me. And I know you bought that expensive ass bed with the changing table attached!" she said while rolling her neck reaching for the door to her room.

"Um, who are you?" Mel looked back at the door to ensure she came into the right room.

"Oh, my name is Terrance," a tall, bright, wavy, dark haired male said.

"And how are you, or better question, why are you here?" Mel questioned.

"Mel, watch it, he may be her family," Syd saying grabbing Mel's arm.

"Nope, the trick said she ain't have no family, so again who are you?" Mel turned rolling her neck and pointing directly in his face.

"Well, it may be a bit hard to expla….." he began speaking just as the door opened

"Hey, new parents," Syd said greeting Damion and Shamika, walking over to hug Damion.

"Wow, you're really getting out there. I know you're going to miss that size two when that baby comes," Shamika said with a slight laugh not noticing her visitor.

"Oh, yeah, hopefully I'll bounce right back," Syd commented back. "Hey, you where's the bundle of joy? Looking for the new baby. You had a vaginal birth?"

"Yeah, hurt like hell, think she tore my ass or something," Shamika said rubbing the bottom of her stomach.

"Oh, wow that was a lot of information," Mel said rolling her eyes. "Why are you so quiet new daddy?" Mel asked Damion.

"Because, I don't understand something," he said apparently trying to keep his composure.

"What's that?" Syd asked

"How you can have a 100% healthy, FULL term, Hispanic baby, when we were just six months pregnant? I am my skin tone and there is no noticeable anything wrong," Damion said slowly raising his voice. "And to top it all off; who the fuck is this dude?"

"I think I will be leaving now," Syd said trying to back out of the door and push Mel as she went.

"NO we ain't. I want to hear what she got to say," Mel said popping her lips.

"So, what you trying to say? I am a liar or something?" Shamika said wincing trying to sit up in the bed, trying not to make eye contact with Terrance.

"Well, if my math is correct, you are a liar and a cheater, so where are you and your child going to go when you leave here?" Damion asked in a calm tone. "Matter of fact, uh, say bruh, what's yo name?"

"Terrance," Mel said as if it were her own name.

Shamika sat there just staring at him, like she didn't recognize him.

"Damion," Syd said feeling her hurt, "What, I mean why, would you say that? You love this lady. You want to marry her? Where did that come from? Who are you right now?"

"Don't defend this scank. She never deserved him anyways," Mel said shaking her head.

"You know, Syd, Mel is right. I know you're pregnant. I know who you slept with to get pregnant, and I know you don't want me to know. It's sad I don't see you every day, but I can account for all the men you have slept with," Damion said seriously.

"Well, since you already know, congratulations Damion. Shamika ain't yo baby momma. So how you feel now?" Mel asked Damion looking at Syd.

"Mel, please shut up, please," Syd begged with tears in her eyes.

"Why she got to shut up? Let the bitch talk," Shamika said.

"Why don't you get acclimated with your child's father and shut the fuck up!"

"Ay, "Terrance said still sitting in there, not moving an inch.

Mel began laughing loudly. "I'll be your bitch today. Hell, obviously he will, too, but no matter what, you can't make him your baby's daddy," she said pointing at Damion.

"I'm gone whoop ya ass!" Shamika said attempting to get up.

"Bay, don't move," Terrance said hurrying to her side.

Mel began to laugh hysterically. "You know I made a promise, but I am sorry Syd," Mel said looking at me. "Damion cheer up, you only have about five more months to go, and then you'll be a great father."

"I hate you, Mel," Syd said leaving, swiftly walking out the room.

Mel attempted to grab her arm. She turned around and said, "We are no longer friends. I hope that one up was worth it."

"You liar, piece of shit. There was nothing going on. How could you lie? What about us," she said snatching away from her real child's father, Shamika started yammering on.

"Shut up, trick. They belong to each other. You..." Mel said walking close to Shamika's face, waving her finger, "you were just a fling gone wrong, but looks like you fixed that though," Mel said placing her pointer finger on Shamika's nose.

Shamika attempted to grab Mel, but was interrupted by a low deep voice.

"Leave her alone Mel. Where is Syd," I need to talk to her. Damion said gathering his things to walk out.

"You right, I hurt my girl," Mel sucked her teeth. "Fuck you trick," she said as she pushed Shamika upside her head and walked out of the room.

"Where is the elevator?" Syd thought pushing the button for the millionth time. She started dialing Greg. "Please answer." She heard Damion and Mel talking and walking in her direction. "I have to get out of here. The elevator is still two floors away. If I don't find a way to my car soon I'm going to jump out this window," she thought to herself. "Exit, where is an exit? Stairs!" She pushed the door and down the stairs she went as fast as her legs would carry her.

"Hello, hello? Babe is everything alright? Hello?" she heard in a faint tone.

She pulled the phone up to her ear. "Babe where are you?" she asked in a winded voice as she approach the second floor.

"Where do you need me to be? What's wrong? Are you okay? What are you doing? Why do you sound like that?" he asked concerned.

"I am trying to get to my car." She hit the automatic start on her car as she get closer to the doors of the hospital but it didn't work. She tried again successfully.

"Babe, where are you? What's going on?" Greg asked again.

"Give me a second," she said feeling winded. She jumped in the car, tossed her phone on the passenger seat, while it connected to the Bluetooth. She pulled the gear into reverse, stepped on the gas, slammed on the break looking down to pull the gear into drive, slammed on the gas again. There was a loud bump under the front of the car. She couldn't see because her eyes were filled with tears. She heard Damion in the distance.

"Please, stop! You're going to kill her. Stop the car please," Damion said yelling into my driver side window, banging on the glass.

"Babe, what was that? What's going on? Where are you? Stop, where you are? I am coming to get you. Talk to me," Greg reasoned.

Syd put the car in park. Too much was happening, and she couldn't control her emotion. Her head started spinning. "What's going on?" Everything started getting dark. "I'm at the Women's Hospital," she tried to yell. Then, nothing…

"Wake up, wake up," she heard Damion yelling. "Oh my God, somebody help us!!!"

Syd heard the passenger window break; she still couldn't see or move. "What's going on?" She heard sirens.

"Mel, wake up! Wake up! This can't be happening!" Damion yelled.

Syd could hear Greg in the distance.

"Sir, please stay behind the line," an unfamiliar voice said.

"That's my wife. She's pregnant, and I have to get to her," Greg begged.

"Mel, nooooo! Please wake, up. I can't lose all of you guys in a day. What did I do to deserve this?" Damion said through sobs.

"What's happening?" Syd wanted to scream. "What's wrong with Mel?" Her head started pounding and it became hard to breathe; darkness, again.

The Hospital after the Accident

"Mel, get up. What the hell? Damn, why wouldn't you tell me? How did we let this get here?" Damion asked as she lay in the hospital bed.

"Look, she hit me with a car and you over here grilling me. The fuck wrong with you?" Mel said grimacing from the pain in her back.

"I know, that was messed up. I am talking about me and you though," Damion said looking her in the eye. "You know how I felt about Shamika and her baby. Why wouldn't you tell me though, Mel? Now she about to marry some other nigga. That is if she makes it out the hospital," he said sitting back in his chair putting his head in his hands.

"Wait, what? Why is she in the hospital? She was driving a car. NOTHING happened to her," Mel said looking like "boy please."

"Well, apparently, she has been stressing out throughout the pregnancy and has been a high risk from the start. Now, she's down there unresponsive, something about blood pressure, toxic something. Look, at the rate my day is going I'm next. Shit, I need a drink."

"Bitch, get up with yo faking ass. You know you okay," a loud deep male voice said walking into the room.

"Ugh, if I could you know I would," Mel said shifting her eyes from Damion to Alex. "Where is Shawn?"

"Honey, he can't take it. He sitting in the waiting area with Syd's mom and dad spilling the tea, you know, they didn't even know she was pregnant, let alone by Damion." Alex said, placing his hands on Damion' shoulders. "So I hear a double congratulation is in order."

Damion got up, took a deep breathe, and said, "She'll tell you. She seems to have all the news and reporting live. I’m going to check on Chryssany," he said walking out of the door.

"Soooo, how you know Damion was her 'baby daddy?"” Mel asked.

"Shawn has been paying close attention to all the situations around us, and obviously we too damn clueless to see all the signs" he said. "Miss Thang gets nervous around him. Even when she was hiding it, he picked up on. I just agreed with my boo, and you just confirmed, chil’," he said waving his hand and rolling his eyes.

"You are a mess and I guess Shawn is more perceptive than I thought," Mel said.

"So is you really hurt or you just doing an insurance claim?" he said laughing but oh so serious.

"Bitch, a little of both I knew I hurt her damn feelings, but hitting me with a car? Wait til I get up. I’m gone beat the brakes off her lil ass," Mel said upset and dismayed.

"Pump yo brakes, bitch. She down there in a coma or something. Blood pressure sky high and some pregnant shit, I tuned out. So whoop her ass after baby Alex gets here."

"What, who the hell is, you know what you play too much. Go check on Syd. I’m okay," Mel said as her eyes shifted from Alex to her door.

Alex turned around shocked. "Oh, okay. What's up, Tino?" he said with too much attitude as he walked out of the room. "I will keep you informed, Miss Bitch."

"Hey, "Valentino said." How's it going?"

"It's going," Mel said smiling looking up at him.

"I could kill Syd for doing this to you," he said getting misty eyed.

"Don't blame her. I told Damion he was her baby daddy in front of Shamika, right after they found out he wasn't Shamika's baby daddy. Drama I know right, but I had to put that smart mouth bitch in her place."

"Damn, I thought with money, y'all ghetto asses would get some class, but y'all still a bunch of niggas. Playing all grown up," he said lifting his cap and rubbing his forehead.

"Yeah, you can take the nigga out the hood, but you can't take the hood out the nigga," Mel agreed.

"Chryssany, are you okay?" G whispered into her ear.

"Yeah, where's Mel?" she asked him in a low, sullen tone.

"She is stable babe," he answered." I will be right back. I am going to get the nurse to let her know you are awake," he said standing, releasing her hand.

"Syd, I kind of figured this was my child growing inside you, but I couldn't be sure without your validity,"

Damion said standing, walking towards the bed not waiting for her to fall back asleep. "Do you love me, like honest whole hearted love, I need to know right now Syd?" Damion said leaning over her bed and staring in her far away eyes.

"Yes, you know the way I feel about you, but we just can’t get it right. When I need and want you, you are busy loving someone else," she said in a weak distant voice.

"I need and want you all the time. You know this. You always have this blockade up, and it’s hard trying to knock it down every time you feel unsure," he explained to her.

"Look, right now I need to know where Mel is, and how she is, and who’s with her if you are here. Please don’t say Valentino. They don’t really get along and I need her to be okay. My head is starting to hurt, ugh, bad, like really bad." Tears begin to fill her eyes and no more words escaped her lips. The baby monitor flat lined and she went limp. He could only fall onto his knees. The one woman he had loved all of his life, and his first child. "God why? His alleged son was a great deal, too. He was his driving purpose. Now, here he was again in the beginning, living, loving, and placing his heart in her hands. "Why me, God ?" he prayed as the tears fell onto Syd’s hospital sheets.

"What happened? She was just awake. What did you do?" Greg sobbed at Damion with nurses rushing in and out of the room.

"We have to get her blood pressure under control; she's seemingly holding her breath and putting her child in distress," one nurse said to the other. "Excuse me sir, what happened? Was she coming around?" she asked hurriedly.

"She just asked about her friend, nothing major," Greg whispered through a clinched jaw. "What did you say to her? What did you do," he looked at D with hurt, pain, and disbelief in his eyes.

"I just asked her questions about our child and our life together," he said looking at the floor, hoping he was not the reason this is happening.

"I am going to need you two to remain calm," the nurse said as they both walked towards the elevator.

"Let me explain something to you, yes she loves you. I know that, but I also know, you chose someone else, and hurt her tremendously. Why can't you leave her alone? She needs me and I her. You see, I had to get in a proper position to be what she needed. Yes I was single, but I was a broken man when I first tried with her. So we went our separate ways, I NEVER once forgot the person I could have hurt so bad, and been so wrong for. I knew my divorce left me broken and to jump into something with such a woman would have ended in flames. You think hearing about your barbeque was by chance? No, I have been looking for an opportunity to run into her. I need this woman. She informed me she was pregnant by you. Yes, I was disturbed, but we had just left a barbeque for you and your fiancée. So, I have accepted the fact that she's having a child, and we have already discussed her and I parenting our child. You don't have time for her. Let me love this woman like she needs to be," Greg said pacing in the front of the elevators. "Where have you been with the parenting classes, the morning sickness, the sleepless nights, all the hospital visits, the nights spent at the hospital? Oh yeah, you were with the other woman, so don't give me that bull about you and her. There is no you and her, only her and I."

"Ay, first this 'y'all' shit ain't gone fly. She been mine since the eighth grade. I fought for her then and now ain't no different. I can't let my best friend end up with someone who don't feel for her like I do. Yeah, I got shit going on, but she always knows she's my number one. Like real talk she no ain't nobody gone take her spot," Damion said looking G square in the eyes. "She will always be mine 'til death, and even then I plan to meet her in heaven because we were meant for each other."

Pushing the button G said, "That's where you're wrong bro. She's your NUMBER one and she will be my ONLY one. You had a diamond and treated her like a rock. She would have done or been anything you needed, but you chose someone who was looking for a come up. How you think that went over in her mind?" The elevator doors opened. Without looking back Greg stepped in and dropped his head. "I need her. You just want her," he said as the doors closed.

As Damion turned to take the steps, he saw a familiar wheelchair, but his heart was too heavy to even call out.

"Wake up. I am okay, and you hit me with a fucking car. I need to sue yo ass. Lady wake up, I am sorry for spilling, but the bitch needed to know you are his one true love. Ratchery aside, I need you Syd, and this kid, to make us a real family. You my main bitch, my sister, and the one person who knows all my faults and still loves me. Seriously, I kept calling your phone I know it was an accident. I know you have been stressed. I just didn't know how much. After that week you took off away from us, I knew you was my girl. Hell, I was waiting on my main ringtone every day. We share everything. Nothing comes between us. Even that petty ass shit that happened right after high school, you and I put that shit aside and made things right. Baby girl, I been protecting you, or so it seemed, since day one of this sisterhood, but you have been my guiding light. Man, Syd just wake up," Mel pleaded.

Syd was unresponsive still in a coma like state.

"Chile, since you 'can't' hear me anyways, why is Damion trying to make Greg leave you alone? I know right," she said as if Syd actually responded. "He talking about you have been his number one, but G wasn't having it, had a dramatic exit and everything. Honey, he said in the deepest voice she could muster, 'There is your problem. You want her as your number one, but I need her as my only one.' He is so sweet and corny," she said just as tickled as she wanted to be.

A tear rolled down Syd's face. "I love you Mel, and I sincerely apologize," she said in almost a whisper. She slowly opened her eyelids, which felt like they weighed a ton. As the room came into focus, her eyes landed on Mel, who was sitting in a tricked out wheelchair. "What the hell? Why Jesus? Is this permanent?" she breathed the words out.

"Calm, sister chic, you are so dramatic," she began snapping her finger in Syd's face. Stay with me boo. No, it isn't permanent. You hear me, lady? Calm down, Syd don't make me stand. My hip hurts, bad as hell, but I will shake that baby right out of your ass!"

She couldn't help but smile. "Thank you, Jesus, for her," Syd thought. "It is very hard for me to talk for some reason, but I am elated. I thought the worst. I want to jump out the bed wrap my arms around her, sit in her lap and plant the wettest kiss on her cheeks and forehead. Ten years and she's still my ride or die (literally)." She just grasped Mel's hand and held on as tight as she could.

"Your mom and dad are here. They, for some reason, were shocked to know you are pregnant, and almost five months. 'Lucy, you have some explaining to do.' They also congratulated D on y'all engagement. I heard he dropped his head and walked away. Alex explained everything to your parents, yes everything. I have to leave before they notice I am not on my floor anymore, but I love you and I humbly accept your apology. Plus, I didn't see malice when you were driving. I saw a lost, scared little girl with a faraway look, crying and driving." She released her hand and rolled out of the room.

In walked Syd's mom and, "Honey," is all she said. She walked toward the bed rubbed and kissed Syd's forehead. "Look at this mess you have made with your life. Is this why you don't keep in touch?" she lectured.

"Michelle," his deep soothing voice rounded the corner, "the child has been through enough without you badgering her. Hey, baby girl," her dad said.

"She hit Melony with a car Michael; I am trying to figure out why she is even in the hospital," her mom said unapologetically.

"Bye, Michelle, Go to the waiting area," he guided her out of the room. "I am sorry, baby girl, but I have a few questions of my own. Are you ready darling?"

She shook her head yes.

"Well, I thought we were close, right?" he questioned?

Again, she shook her head yes.

"Well, why wouldn't you call Daddy before things got out of hand? I have always been there to help and protect you. I will always take your side. You are my only daughter, and that's why I was put here, to keep you safe," he said in a firm voice.

Her eyes began to water, but she was still very speechless.

"Awww, darling don't cry. I didn't mean to hurt your feelings. Syd, you can always talk to me about anything. I am always here for you," he said leaning in to hug her. "You are still my snuggle bug. I don't care if you are 128!"

She smiled. "I love you, Daddy," she whispered.

"Okay, let me go. I know your mom is in there questioning all of your friends. We went to see Mel, and she wasn't in her room."

She smiled again. "She'll be there now."

The nurse entered with a pitcher of water. "Your vitals are looking strong, and if we can keep you awake for eight hours or more you will be clear to leave. Your daughter is doing well also. She seems to be a real trooper."

"Wait, what?" Syd asked puzzled. "There is a girl in there? How can you tell is it not still too early to tell? I thought I was only six or seven weeks. Sweetie you are a bit further than that. Your OBGYN will be in to visit with you in the next hour. Your fiancée requested that he personally check on your child. Do you have any questions for me?"

"No," she said drinking the water as quickly as she could.

"Okay, call me if you need me," she said as she walked out the door.

"Hey, Becky," Syd called, "have you seen my fiancée recently?"

"Yes, a few hours ago," she said with a faraway look on her face, as if she were still thinking.

"Thank you again," Syd said.

The Party

"Baby, I want to take you somewhere special, tonight, so get your things and meet me at the car in 5 minutes," G said walking out of the bedroom.

"Okay, babe, but what about the banquet? Are we not going?" Syd said following him with a six month pregnant belly.

"No, just meet me in the car," he said demanding.

"Is this because, I'm pregnant?" Syd said with the worst attitude.

"No, it's because I love you and I want to take you somewhere nice, that's all. Is that okay with you, Miss Lady?" he asked smiling that wonderful smile of his as he walked out. "Now, please get finished. I'm going to get the car."

She put her final touches on, her earrings, made sure there were no stray curls, her perfume, and a quick glance in the mirror. She smiled and dashed out the room, down the stairs, and out the door. He pulled up to the front door to pick her up, and locked the house with his universal remote. Can you get in? Do you need some help?" he asked walking around his all white Porsche 911 GT3.

"Yes and no," she laughed.

He grasped her arm and he helped her into the car.

"G, honey I just noticed I hadn't talked to any of my friends in a few days. Do you think it was something I said or did? Wow, it's not like any of them to not call. I know I haven't called, so it's probably just me I'll call them tomorrow," she said resolving her own situation.

"See baby girl, you really don't need me. That's why I have to hurry up and marry you before you figure that out," he said side-eyeing her.

She smiled and looked out the window to survey the surroundings. "We're almost there," she said excitedly, wanting some salmon.

"Yes we are honey," he said turning on o Germantown Road. He pulled into the parking lot, and there was a spot right at the door.

"The place looks packed, honey. Are you sure? I feel a bit overdressed. Are you sure you want to eat here?" she whined.

"Chryssany, get out the car and let's go in. Stop worrying. You look great and I told you we have reservations," he reassured her.

They walked into the restaurant. He motioned for the Maître D. "Mr. Thornton, I presume?" she asked.

"Your presumption is correct," he verified.

"Right this way. I have your table ready." She walked them over to a raised area and had a waiter to come give Syd a hand getting up there.

"Aww, thank you so much," she said.

"My name is Stephanie. I'll be serving you today, and may I get you some drinks?"

"Yes, please. May I have pineapple juice mixed with cranberry juice, with a water, no ice please?" Syd ordered.

"I'll have the same, hold the cranberry and water." G said. "Thank you."

"So what's the special occasion?" Syd said starting a conversation.

"I can't just treat the woman in my life to something she enjoys?" he said with that smile of his. "Can I ask you something, honey?"

"Sure, shoot," she said prepared for anything

"Chryssany Michelle Jackson, can you promise me, when you're ready to leave you'll tell me and won't just up and leave? When the love starts wearing off, you'll tell me? When you need a friend, you'll call me? When you need affection, you'll show me? When you're not having such a good day, even if it's my fault, you'll tell me? When you find someone better suited for you, you'll tell me? When you miss me, you will tell me?

When you love me, when you dislike me, when you feel you've had enough or just a little too much, would you please tell me?" G asked looking her into her eyes, wanting their souls to meet as if it were the first time.

"I promise, under one condition," she said waving her pointer finger to draw his attention away from her eyes for a split second.

"What's that, queen?" he said.

"You do the same for me," she said planting an immense, moist kiss on his beautiful bodacious lips.

"I do," he said pulling away. "Baby, I have another question."

"Okay, honey, hit me," she said wanting to get back to the loving.

"Will you do me a huge favor and make me the happiest man on earth, by becoming Mrs. Gregory Thornton? I lost you once I can't do it again," he said pulling out a 4 carat ring and replacing the one she had previously worn on her finger.

It fits, she thought. "Yes, baby, I will. I do. Wow, YES."

Just as she said yes the people in the restaurant all began to stand and clap. Her best friends were all there, her mother, father, and his parents.

"You did all this for me, baby?" she said with tears of joy running down her face.

"Congratulations, girl! I don't know how much longer we could have sat there and not said anything to you," Shawn said.

"Shawn, Alex, Mel, Damion, HEY!!! I'm getting married," Syd said still in disbelief.

"We know. We've known for a little while now. That's why we couldn't keep in touch," Alex said.

"Yo man rented the whole place out and invited your family, friends, and everyone you inherited through marriage," Mel, explained.

"Oh, my goodness! I gotta go. Be right back," Syd said with the sudden urge to pee.

They were all still talking and she had on too many clothes to be quick. Once she entered the bathroom, she checked to make sure there was no one to help her hold her dress and there wasn't. So she went into the largest stall and began her journey to pee. She heard the door open and close.

"Um hello, who's there?" she asked knowing she still needed some help.

"It's me, "a man's voice said.

"Damion?" She said at a complete loss for words

"Yeah," he said opening the stall.

"You see this? Isn't it great? I'm getting my happily ever after," she said still excited trying to get back in an upright position.

"Yeah, your happily ever after. He helped her zip her dress and fluff the bottom and followed her to the sink.

"Look, Syd, we were meant to be together. Why are you doing this to me? You're already promised yourself to me," Damion said trying to make her feel bad.

"Well, first of all, a few months ago you were promised to Shamika, and she was IT for you so don't bring this promised crap to me. I'm over that, and you should most definitely be," she said not looking up at him, drying her hands.

"Well, if this is my child let me raise it. Let me be a father to my child. Syd, please don't take this away from me. All we've been through, I need us to work and be together. I want my family. I want you," he said moving a little too close to her face.

"No, Damion. You had your chance and you chose Mika. I don't fault you for that. I just know exactly how to play my cards and how to separate real love from fake lust if you catch my drift," she said still very defensive. "I know what we've been through, and I know that we will never work because of our past. Please don't do this to me right now."

Just tell me what's going on. Why? Why are we not together? Why did we not end up happily ever after?" Damion said pleading with her

"Our happily ever after got cut short when you decided to proposed to someone other than me, Damion.

I have waited and put my love life on hold waiting and hoping that you'd finally realize what a superwoman you had waiting on you. Yet, you always overlooked me until you wanted to be fucked right. My goods are now someone else's goodies, someone who loves and appreciates them twenty-four hours a day, seven days a week," she said tired of his same shit every time.

"Chryssany, not like this. Just tell me what I have to do. Please, I'm begging you to love me again. You're the only one that knows how to make me smile without being around. Just please tell me," Damion said becoming misty eyed.

"Look Damion, I don't want to play step-mother, especially not with Mika's ghetto ass child. Plus this is her space. Then you yourself know that baby isn't yours. Did you just say that to make me feel better, so I would think you were mine to myself? I would have been fine if you never said that, but it's there, Damion. You and I both know it. You can't let her go for some reason or another. I have my own little one to worry about. I want my own family. I don't want to be second in any way. I want my child to be first. I would feel bad if I treated 'your' child differently from my own. Look, I'm sorry, Damion. This just isn't going to work. I'm so sorry," she said unyielding. "Why are you even here trying this? And Shamika is going to pull your string and off you will go, until that guy what's his name? Oh, yeah, Terrance decides to pull hers."

"What your own family should consist of a mother, a father, and a child that the two parents share. And if memory serves me correctly, Greg has a child already, or have you forgotten?" Damion said in a gotcha tone.

"You are impossible. G loves us, me and my child. His child was killed by a drunk driver a few years ago. You two are perfect together. When Shamika sets the date, send me an invitation, and we'll be there. Good day," she said trying to walk out of the restroom. "I don't believe this foolishness. I have wasted my life for you, and this is the thanks I get? I finally find happiness, and you want to take it away from me? Fuck you, Damion," she said pushing him out of the restroom. She grabbed her phone before she walked out, and pressed the number two "*BESTFRIEND.*" The phone began to ring. She opened the door to make eye contact with Mel just as Damion was approaching her.

"Hello, Mrs. Thornton," Mel said in a glowing voice.

"Mel," she said starting to cry and couldn't stop.

"What's wrong honey? Where are you? I'm coming to you now. What happened?" she said scrambling around. She rushed into the bathroom, hanging up the phone.

"What the hell is his deal? This is my freaking kid! What was I not supposed to tell him any of it? He said we were meant to be. What the hell, am I wrong?" she said questioning her own judgment

"No, sweetie. How do you feel? What happened?" Mel asked concerned.

"Mel I know what I said and I meant it, too, but I don't want to raise my child alone. Even G had a child I know, seven or eight years old, that he kept in touch with. I also am not sure that I want this baby. I some days don't want the mother experience because I don't want to mess up another human. Hell, I sometimes don't want a husband because I don't know if this person was meant to be with me or someone else. I used to think Damion was my soul mate, and then I ran into G. He was everything Damion was and some. And I don't want to put Damion's baby on another man because I don't want to live the rest of my life alone. Without some type of companionship, I'll have a child with no father figure in its life. Oh, Mel I don't know what to do. I don't know if it's the baby making my hormones crazy like this or what. All I know is, I once wanted Damion and only him, and now G is making me rethink everything I ever thought about love."

"Well, don't you think that's a great thing? A man that makes you rethink the way you love, and who you love, is a wonderful being, Syd. You know what Damion has, and you also know he wants his cake and eat it, too. I asked him is it possible for a man to love two women because I wanted to understand how he says he loves you, but his actions show totally different. He told me yes he does believe it is possible because one has this one really great trait about her and the other has everything else. So, Syd it’s up to you to decide if you have one really great trait, or everything else, and knowing you, you’ll say everything else. So, honey is he worth waiting for if you have that much to offer?"

"Where he at? Where my baby daddy?" Shamika said looking around. "I know he here and y'all should know he mines."

"Who is that?" Someone asked, "Is she related? Why is she so loud?"

"Look, you classless twit, this isn't about you or even him; leave before I remove you, myself!" Mel, threatened her. "You're not pregnant anymore so please give me a reason."

"Mel, give her who she's looking for," Syd walked out, glowing and seemingly floating. "She wants him. Let’s see if he wants her."

Searching the room for Damion, they spotted him. Syd mouthed to him, "Don't move." He just nodded. "Come on sweetie." Syd grabbed her hand as she sashayed over to him. "Let's see if he wants her like she wants him."

"Honey, leave her be. Come with me. Its picture time. Misery loves company, please watch the company you keep," G said scowling at Shamika.

"Don't worry boo. I got this," Mel said winking at Syd. "Come on, hood rat."

As they approached him, he looked at Shamika. "What do you want? Why are you here? Shamika this is not the place. Where is your child while you're here with me?" Damion asked.

“With the father," she said bluntly.

"OOhhh, wrong answer," Mel said laughing uncontrollably.

"Um, right this way, sexy," Tino said not trying to make eye contact with the situation.

Mel asked trying to stay within ear shot of the conversation, "But, why though? She came to interrupt my girl's day, the least you can do is allow me the satisfaction of him telling her..."

"Look Mika, you a hoe. You know you a hoe, so why are you trying to make me wife you? You don’t have the potential to even try to change. We have tried to salvage what was left, and no sparks only arguments and bad times. Hell, you wouldn’t even bring your son around me. How dare you bring this drama here? That's why we will never work. Get out. As a matter of fact, let me walk you out. You aren’t only embarrassing yourself, you’re embarrassing me," he said grabbing her arm and forcefully removing her. As they approached the door he said plainly, "Stay away from me. You are the worst kind of poison, and you have done all the damage I can take. Stay the fuck back, or next time I won’t be so nice," he said letting the door go on her.

Damion walked back in looking for Syd. After finding her sitting on the outskirts of the picture area, he walked over to her. "Look, Syd we belong together. We were meant to be, remember? I know I messed up time and time again. You always knew I was your end game. Why not now? Why not here? Syd please, just please," he pleaded with her.

"Look, sometimes you have to let go of the things that have let you go. We have been at this for a lifetime and it has yet to work. Why not give up? My ending is with him. He is the embodiment of my dreams. He loves me without bias," she said as her eyes began to tear up from the pain. "Please just leave well enough alone. Live and let live."

"Are you okay?" D asked then noticing her gripping their child.

"I'm okay," she said searching the room for her future husband, dad, or best friend. "Please, somebody," she thought feeling the pain escalate. Her eyes met Mel's. She walked swiftly over to her.

"What did you do to her? You are a true fuck up. Why can't you let her be happy? Why do you have to hurt her every fucking time? I asked you to stay away before your miserable ass, lonely she dog, delivered her bastard child, but you just don't listen. You just do whatever you want. You truly can't give a fuck about my friend," she said grabbing Chryssany, trying to support her weight.

"Queen, what happened? What's wrong," G said. "What did you do?" he asked grabbing Damion. "You can't help but hurt her. Go home to your hood rat. Leave my queen alone," and he shoved Damion away. "Baby are you, okay? Is it the baby, Syd? SYD, baby. Please."

"Baby, I'm fine," Syd said in a faint voice. "See?" she said trying to smile and make light of the situation.

"Come on, Syd. Let's get you in the car," Mel said coaxing her friend to the car.

Another pain hit her. Syd began to hold her breath as her head started to swim, the sweat forming on her nose.

"Syd, stay awake," Mel said as she walked her to the door, as Tino drove up in her truck. "Please be okay," she said as her tears began to fill her eyes.

"She will be. She has to," G said as he placed his future wife gently in the car observing her chest slowly rising and falling, slower than usual. "That can't be the best," he thought as the hurt began to fill his heart. "I can't lose her. I just got her back. Not like this. Please get her to the hospital soon," he begged Tino as he closed the door behind him.

"I'm going with you," a dark deep voice said as he snatched the door back open.

"If you don't get the fuck away from my car, there will be a funeral and a wedding, you selfish inconsiderate bastard. You did this," Mel said as she motioned for Tino to drive off.

Tino said, "Sorry man," and hit the gas leaving Damion standing there in his misery.

Damion watched Alex and Shawn drive passed without a second thought. He just stood there, mind racing, body unable to, but his unborn child and the love of his life that he may never get a chance to fix were in trouble.

Syd's parent's pulled up in their Cadillac CTS V-Sport and unlocked the doors. Damion steps in, her mom had no words. Her father simply stated, "I don't know the situation son, but if that's your child like they say, you should be a part, but if you cause her any more hurt, I will cause you the same." He put the car in gear and drove off. They rode in silence. As they approached the ER, he let them out at the door, went and parked. They all rushed in, as they found her being rushed into the back.

"I'm her husband; I'll go back with her," G said without any hesitation.

"That's my child. I need to be sure they are okay," Damion hurriedly said as they walked back.

The nurse simply stated, "There are two visitors allowed, so right this way," as they took her to the back. They began to undress her and hook her up to the monitors. G noticed her breathing seemingly had stopped, and she had become lifeless.

"What's going on? Is she breathing?" G said as the tears began to fall down his face.

Damion noticed the contractions also had come to an end; he could no longer see the imprint of his unborn child. "Why is the baby not moving?" he began sobbing.

After hooking her up to the machines, the nurse began putting the two men out of the room, as they were leaving they only heard,

"WE HAVE NO HEARTBEAT…."

www.ingramcontent.com/pod-product-compliance
Lightning Source LLC
Chambersburg PA
CBHW061426040426
42450CB00007B/923

9780692408049